Family Ideas

for Ministry with Young Teens

Heads-up | Easy | Low-Cost | Purposeful

Family Ideas

for Ministry with Young Teens

Carole Goodwin

Heads-up | Easy | Low-Cost | Purposeful

Saint Mary's Press
Christian Brothers Publications
Winona, Minnesota

For my parents

Genuine recycled paper with 10% post-consumer waste.
Printed with soy-based ink.

The publishing team included Marilyn Kielbasa, development editor; Mary Duerson, copy editor; Barbara Bartelson, production editor; Hollace Storkel, typesetter; Cindi Ramm, art director; Kenneth Hey, cover and logo designer; cover images, PhotoDisc Inc.; produced by the graphics division of Saint Mary's Press.

The development consultants for the HELP (Heads-up, Easy, Low-Cost, and Purposeful) series included the following people:

Sarah Bush, Pewee Valley, Kentucky

Jeanne Fairbanks, Tipp City, Ohio

Carole Goodwin, Louisville, Kentucky

Joe Grant, Louisville, Kentucky

Maryann Hakowski, Belleville, Illinois

Jo Joy, Temple, Texas

Kevin Kozlowski, New Carlisle, Ohio

Jennifer MacArthur, Cincinnati, Ohio

David Nissen, Cincinnati, Ohio

Ruthie Nonnenkamp, Prospect, Kentucky

The acknowledgments continue on page 114.

Printed in the United States of America

Printing: 9 8 7 6 5 4 3 2 1

Year: 2008 07 06 05 04 03 02 01 00

ISBN 0-88489-574-2

Library of Congress Cataloging-in-Publication Data

Goodwin, Carole
Family ideas for ministry with young teens / Carole Goodwin.
        p. cm. — (HELP)
ISBN 0-88489-574-2
1. Church work with teenagers—Catholic Church. 2. Church work with families—Catholic Church.
I. Title. II. HELP (Series : Winona, Minn.)
BX2347.8.Y7 G657   2000
249—dc21

99-050983

Contents

Introduction

Family Ideas for Ministry with Young Teens is one of seven books in the HELP series—a collection of **H**eads-up, **E**asy, **L**ow-Cost, and **P**urposeful activities for young adolescents. These strategies are designed to be used as part of a comprehensive youth ministry program for grades six to eight. The strategies can stand alone or complement a religious education curriculum.

The other books in the HELP series are as follows:
- *Community-Building Ideas for Ministry with Young Teens* (available in 2001)
- *Hands-on Ideas for Ministry with Young Teens* (available in 2001)
- *Holiday and Seasonal Ideas for Ministry with Young Teens*
- *Justice and Service Ideas for Ministry with Young Teens*
- *Prayer Ideas for Ministry with Young Teens*
- *Retreat Ideas for Ministry with Young Teens* (available in 2001)

These books are helpful resources for anyone who works with young adolescents in a church or school setting. They can provide a strong foundation for a year-round, total youth ministry program whose goal is to evangelize young adolescents and support them in their faith journey.

Overview of This Book

Family Ideas for Ministry with Young Teens may be used by a coordinator of youth ministry, a director of religious education, catechists, teachers, family ministers, a parish youth ministry team, or any adult who works with young teens. Ownership of the book includes permission to duplicate any part of it for use with program participants.

The book's strategies are divided into three categories:

◎ activities for gathered families

◎ activities for families at home

◎ activities for teen groups or classes

Included are ways to foster communication between young teens and parents, to engage young teens and their families in service, to build community among families with young teens, and to attend to the spiritual needs of young adolescents. Note that in activities that involve parents, you may, of course, include guardians, sponsors, or any adult family members who are attending your program with the teens.

Format of the Strategies

Each strategy begins with a brief overview of its purpose. The next element is a suggested time for the activity. This is flexible and takes into account several variables, such as the size of the group, the comfort level of the participants, and whether you want to include a break. Use the suggested time as a starting point and modify it according to your circumstances. It is a good idea to include time for a break within the longer strategies.

Next is a description of the size of the group that the strategy was written for. Most of the strategies work with a range of group sizes.

In some strategies a section on special considerations follows the one on group size. It includes things such as notices about remote preparation requirements and cautions to pay special attention to a particular developmental issue of early adolescence.

A complete checklist of materials needed is the next part of the presentation of every strategy. A detailed description of the strategy's procedure is then provided, followed by alternative approaches. The alternatives may be helpful in adapting the strategy to the needs of the families in your group.

Frequently included is a list of scriptural passages that may be used with the strategy for reflection or prayer. The list is not exhaustive; a Bible concordance will provide additional citations if you want to add a more substantial scriptural component to a strategy.

The final element in each strategy offers space for keeping notes about how you might want to use the strategy in the future or change it to fit the needs of your group.

Programming Ideas

The strategies in this book can be used in a variety of ways. Consider the following suggestions:

◎ The program coordinator, catechists, teachers, family minister, and coordinator of youth ministry may collaborate to plan youth meetings and special activities that use strategies from this and other books in the HELP series.

◎ The strategies in this book may be used anytime during the year. Some activities might best be presented in the summer months, when most young adolescents and their families are less busy and may be open to a variety of activities. Youth ministers may use those strategies as part of a strong summer program for young teens.

◎ School leaders can use ideas from this book to create faith-sharing nights for students in grades six to eight, and their parents.

◎ Many of the strategies from other books in the HELP series can be adapted for use with multigenerational groups.

Standard Materials

Many of the items in the materials checklists are common to several strategies in the series. To save time consider gathering frequently used materials in convenient bins and storing those bins in a place that is accessible to all staff and volunteer leaders. Some recommendations for how to organize such bins follow.

Supply Bin

The following items frequently appear in materials checklists:

◎ Bibles, at least one for every two participants
◎ masking tape
◎ cellophane tape
◎ washable and permanent markers (thick and thin)
◎ pens or pencils
◎ self-stick notes
◎ scissors
◎ newsprint
◎ blank paper, scrap paper, and notebook paper
◎ postcards
◎ notepaper
◎ envelopes
◎ baskets
◎ candles and matches
◎ items to create a prayer space (e.g., a colored cloth, a cross, a bowl of water, and a vase for flowers)

Craft Bin

Many of the strategies use craft activities to involve the young people. Consider collecting the following supplies in a separate bin:

◎ construction paper
◎ yarn and string, in assorted colors

- poster board
- glue and glue sticks
- fabric paints
- glitter and confetti
- used greeting cards
- beads
- modeling clay
- paintbrushes and paints
- crayons
- used magazines and newspapers
- hole punches
- scissors
- stickers of various kinds
- index cards
- gift wrap and ribbon

Music Bin

Young people often find deep and profound meaning in the music and lyrics of songs, both past and present. Also, the right music can set an appropriate mood for a prayer or activity. Begin with a small collection of tapes or CDs in a music bin and add to it over time. You might ask the young people to put some of their favorite music in the bin. The bin might include the following styles of music:

- *Fun gathering music that is neither current nor popular with young teens.* Ideas are well-known classics (e.g., *Overture to William Tell, Stars and Stripes Forever,* and *1812 Overture*), songs from musical theater productions, children's songs, and Christmas songs for use any time of the year.
- *Prayerful, reflective instrumental music, such as the kind that is available in the adult alternative, or New Age, section of music stores.* Labels that specialize in this type of music include Windham Hill and Narada.
- *Popular songs with powerful messages.* If you are not well versed in popular music, ask the young people to offer suggestions.
- *The music of contemporary Christian artists.* Most young teens are familiar with Amy Grant, Michael W. Smith, and Steven Curtis Chapman. Also include the work of Catholic musicians, such as David W. Kauffman, Steve Angrisano, Bruce Deaton, Sarah Hart, Jesse Manibusan, and Jessica Alles.

Other Helpful Resources

In addition to the seven books in the HELP series, the following resources can be useful in your ministry with young adolescents. All the books in the following list are published by Saint Mary's Press and can be obtained by calling or writing us at the phone number and address listed in the "Your Comments or Suggestions" section at the end of this introduction.

The Catholic Youth Bible, edited by Brian Singer-Towns (2000). The most youth-friendly Bible for Catholic teens available. The scriptural text is accompanied by hundreds of articles to help young people pray, study, and live the Scriptures.

Faith Works for Junior High: Scripture- and Tradition-Based Sessions for Faith Formation, by Lisa-Marie Calderone-Stewart (1993). A series of twelve active meeting plans on various topics related to the Scriptures and church life.

Guided Meditations for Junior High: Good Judgment, Gifts, Obedience, Inner Blindness, by Jane E. Ayer (1997). Four guided meditations for young teens, available on audiocassette or compact disc. A leader's guide includes the script and programmatic options. Other volumes in this series, called A Quiet Place Apart, will also work with young teens.

Looking Past the Sky: Prayers by Young Teens, edited by Marilyn Kielbasa (1999). A collection of 274 prayers by and for young adolescents in grades six to eight.

One-Day Retreats for Junior High Youth, by Geri Braden-Whartenby and Joan Finn Connelly (1997). Six retreats that each fit into a school day or an afternoon or evening program. Each retreat contains a variety of icebreakers, prayers, group exercises, affirmations, and guided meditations.

Prayers with Pizzazz for Junior High Teens, by Judi Lanciotti (1996). A variety of creative prayer experiences that grab young teens' attention. The prayers are useful in many different settings, such as classes, meetings, prayer services, and retreats.

ScriptureWalk Junior High: Bible Themes, by Maryann Hakowski (1999). Eight 90-minute sessions to help bring youth and the Bible together. Each session applies biblical themes to the life issues that concern young teens.

Catechism Connection for Teens collection, by Lisa Calderone-Stewart and Ed Kunzman (1999).

> *That First Kiss and Other Stories*
> *My Wish List and Other Stories*
> *Better Than Natural and Other Stories*
> *Straight from the Heart and Other Stories*
> *Meeting Frankenstein and Other Stories*

> The five books in this collection contain short, engaging stories for teens on the joys and struggles of adolescent life, each story with a reflection connecting it to a Catholic Christian belief. Each book's faith connections reflect teachings from a different part of the *Catechism of the Catholic Church.*

Connections to the Discovering Program

The Discovering Program, published by Saint Mary's Press, is a religious education program for young people in grades six to eight. It consists of fourteen six-session minicourses. Each session is 1 hour long and based on the principles of active learning.

The strategies in the HELP series cover themes that are loosely connected to those explored by the Discovering Program, and can be used as part of a total youth ministry program in which the Discovering curriculum is the central catechetical component. However, no strategy in the series presumes that the participants have taken a particular course in the Discovering Program, or requires that they do so. The appendices at the end of this book list the connections between the HELP strategies and the Discovering courses.

Your Comments or Suggestions

Saint Mary's Press wants to know your reactions to the strategies in the HELP series. We are also interested in new youth ministry strategies for use with young teens. If you have a comment or suggestion, please write the series editor, Marilyn Kielbasa, at 702 Terrace Heights, Winona, MN 55987-1320; call the editor at our toll-free number, 800-533-8095; or e-mail the editor at *mkielbasa@smp.org.* Your ideas will help improve future editions of these books.

Part A

Strategies
for Gathered Families

The following strategies are designed for a gathering of families. Invite the young teens and their families to meet at the same place and time to enjoy the activities together. The strategies are designed for the parents *and* the youth.

Dare to Share

OVERVIEW

This strategy invites the families to play a game that can help them gain knowledge about their family members, and identify events, values, and practices that are special to their family.

Suggested Time

30 to 45 minutes

Group Size

This strategy can be done with two to ten family teams of two to three people each.

Special Considerations

Young people whose family members are not present, or other unattached participants, can be assigned the role of game helper. You will need a game director, a judge, a bell ringer, a timekeeper, and a spotlight holder.

Materials Needed

- 3-by-5-inch index cards, one for each person
- pens or pencils
- newsprint and a marker
- stick-on name tags, one for each person
- colored markers
- a coin

☼ a lectern or a music stand
☼ a handbell
☼ a flashlight
☼ a stopwatch, or a watch or clock with a second hand
☼ strips of colored ribbon, approximately 3-by-5 inches, one for each family

PROCEDURE

Preparation. Before the meeting make an award for every family by writing, "We dare to share!" on a wide strip of ribbon, about 3-by-5 inches. Place a lectern or a music stand at the front of the room. In front of that arrange two facing rows of three chairs each. And beyond those chairs place a table and chairs facing the front of the room for a judge, a timekeeper, a bell ringer, and a spotlight holder.

Finally, write the following questions on a piece of newsprint and post it where everyone can see it easily:

1. Who is your best friend?
2. What is your favorite food?
3. What is the most fun you have had on a family vacation or outing?
4. What is an important Christmas tradition that your family enjoys?
5. How does your family celebrate birthdays?
6. What is one way your family prays together?
7. If your parents won $30,000 in a lottery, what would they most likely do with the money?
8. What topic or issue does your family most often argue about?
9. What is the favorite leisure time activity of the teenager or teenagers in your family?
10. What is the favorite leisure time activity of your parent whose birthday is closest to yours?

1. As the participants arrive, invite any unattached teens or extra participants to be game helpers. You will need a game director, a timekeeper, a bell ringer, a judge, and a spotlight holder. Explain their tasks to them, as described below. You may want to recruit another adult to do this briefing because you will need to greet and instruct families as soon as they arrive (see below).

2. Also as people arrive, separate family members and caution them not to talk to one another. Give everyone a 3-by-5-inch index card and a pen or pencil. Invite them to write their name at the top of their card, list the numbers 1 to 10 down the left-hand side, and write the answer to each posted question by its corresponding number.

3. Distribute blank stick-on name tags and colored markers and tell the participants to write the last name of their teen participant in large letters on their name tag and to put it on so that all the other participants can see it easily.

4. While the families are making their name tags, instruct the judge to collect the index cards and stack the cards from each family in a separate pile. (For example, the cards that belong to the Anderson family should be stacked together.) Explain to the judge that his or her role during the game will be to check the responses when a family spokesperson answers the questions.

5. Assemble the large group of families to form an audience for the game. Tell them to sit beyond the judge's table, facing the front of the room. Encourage them to cheer and applaud when correct responses are given and to moan when incorrect responses are given.

Have the game director invite two families to come forward and sit in the two facing rows of chairs, one family on each side. Then tell the game director to flip a coin to determine which family may begin. Have that family choose a spokesperson and invite her or him to come to the lectern or music stand and prepare to answer the posted questions.

Explain to everyone that teenage spokespeople are to answer the questions as they think their parent or parents answered, and adult spokespeople are to answer the questions as they think their child or children answered. For example, when the game director asks Mrs. Anderson, "How did your child answer the question, Who is your best friend?" and Mrs. Anderson gives the answer that is on her child's card, as determined by the judge, she is correct, the bell ringer rings the bell, and the Anderson family gains a point. She may continue answering questions, up to five correct responses. If the answer is incorrect or if she takes longer than 10 seconds to answer, then Mrs. Anderson sits down and the other team's spokesperson comes to the lectern or music stand. The game director resumes the questioning with the question that was missed. Throughout the game the spotlight holder's task is to shine a flashlight on the spokesperson, and the timekeeper's role is to monitor the time and signal when 10 seconds have passed.

After both teams have had a chance to answer five questions, tally their points. If one team has a higher score, urge the audience to cheer the winners, and invite the two teams to rejoin the audience. If the score is tied, have the game director continue with the unused questions on the posted list. If the tie is not broken by the end of the list, thank the families, have them rejoin the audience, and continue the game with new players.

6. After all the families have competed, give a "We dare to share!" award to every family and declare that everyone is a winner when they learn to communicate better and when they dare to share.

7. Invite everyone to stand in a circle and close with the following prayer or one you create:

> O God, bless these families who are gathered here before you. All the parents want your protection to cover their children like the wings of a mother hen, shielding them from all harm. All the young people want your love to shine through their parents as a model for Christian living. We ask that you grant this protection and this sign of love. May our lives be graced by your presence. We ask this in the name of Jesus, who taught us to love and who lives and reigns with you and the Holy Spirit, one God forever and ever. Amen.

ALTERNATIVE APPROACHES

- Instruct the participants to write each answer on a separate large card or piece of poster board instead of writing all their answers on one 3-by-5-inch card. Tell them to hold up the corresponding card after each question that their family spokesperson answers. This eliminates the role of judge and might make the game more interactive.
- Instead of using the 3-by-5-inch index cards, have the spokesperson escorted out of the room. Then let the remaining family member or members answer the questions verbally. Bring the spokesperson back into the room to answer the questions as he or she thinks the other people in the family answered them.
- Invite the families to brainstorm a list of more questions and have a tournament. You may want to conduct the tournament at another time and finish it with a potluck.

SCRIPTURAL CONNECTIONS

- Deut. 4:9–10 (Teach God's decrees to your children and your children's children.)
- Prov. 23:22–25 (Children should listen to their parents.)
- Eph. 6:1–4 (Children must honor their parents, and parents must train their children.)
- Col. 3:21 (Parents should not nag, lest their children lose heart.)

NOTES

Use the space below to jot notes and reminders for the next time you use this strategy.

What Is That You Said?

This strategy gives parents and young teens a chance to identify some parent statements and teen statements that are commonly used in their families.

Suggested Time

25 to 30 minutes

Group Size

This strategy can be done with four or more families.

Materials Needed

☼ newsprint, two pieces for each small group and an extra piece for the leader
☼ markers, one for each person
☼ masking tape

PROCEDURE

Preparation. Divide a large piece of newsprint into six columns, and label each column with one of the following headings:

◎ Most commonly used parent statements
◎ Most commonly used teen statements
◎ Most unusual parent statements
◎ Most unusual teen statements
◎ Funniest parent statements
◎ Funniest teen statements

1. After the parents and teens arrive, divide the large group into small groups of four to six people each. Do not assign family members to the same group.

Give each group two pieces of newsprint and a marker. Tell the groups each to select a recorder. Have the recorder label the top of one piece of newsprint, "Parent statements," and the top of the other, "Teen statements."

Ask everyone to tell what they think parents might say if every time their young person goes outside, he or she leaves the front door of the house open. Suggest, for example, that a parent might respond: "We don't live in a barn. Close the door." Tell the recorders to list their group's suggested statements under the heading "Parent statements."

Then direct the groups to brainstorm other common parent statements and common teen statements. Invite them to think of situations in their own family life where common statements are used. Remind them that many positive as well as negative statements are used in family contexts. For example, ask what a parent might say when a son or daughter does something that makes a parent extremely proud. Invite the groups to come up with eight to ten sayings for each category. Instruct the recorders to write the sayings on their pieces of newsprint.

Be prepared to suggest phrases such as the following:

◎ "Money does not grow on trees."
◎ "I am not your maid."
◎ "I am bored."
◎ "Everybody is doing it!"
◎ "I love you."
◎ "I am sorry."

Or you might suggest situations to spark their memories:

◎ A son or daughter asks for money to go shopping.
◎ A son or daughter asks to go to the mall.
◎ A parent denies a child permission to do something that other young people get to do.
◎ A teen's parents agree with her or his decision about an important event.

2. After about 10 minutes, gather the small groups. Invite the recorders to tape their lists on a wall at the front of the room and to read through their lists for the large group.

Distribute markers to everyone. Tell them to take a few moments to look over the lists and then do the following:

Put a check mark beside the parent statement and the teen statement that seem to be the most commonly used.

Put a star beside the parent statement and the teen statement that you think are the most unusual.

Put a smile beside the parent statement and the teen statement that you think are the funniest.

3. Assemble the large group and together identify the parent statements that received the most marks for being most commonly used, most unusual, and funniest. Then identify the teen statements that received the most marks in each of those categories. Display the piece of newsprint that you prepared before the meeting. Recruit a volunteer to be a recorder. Tell that person to write under the appropriate heading the parent statements chosen as most commonly used, most unusual, and funniest. Then have him or her write under the appropriate heading the teen statements chosen as most commonly used, most unusual, and funniest.

Lead a discussion using questions like the following:

Is the most commonly used statement of parents positive or negative? Why, do you think, is this so?

Is the most commonly used statement of teens positive or negative? Why, do you think, is this so?

What do the most unusual statements reveal about the people who use them?

How does humor help when situations are tense?

The next time you hear one of these statements in your own family, how do you think you might respond?

4. Gather the young people in a circle facing in. Invite the adults to make a circle around the young people. Tell the adults to extend their hands over the heads of the young people standing in front of them. Invite the young people to bow their head. Share this blessing or make up one or your own:

O God of all goodness, bless these young people who stand before us. May they grow in wisdom and learn to walk in your ways. We ask this in the name of Jesus. Amen.

Invite the young people to turn and face the adults. Tell them to extend their hands over the heads of the adults. Invite the adults to bow their head. Share this blessing or make up one of your own:

> O God of all goodness, bless these adults as they share their wisdom and model how to walk in your ways. We ask this in the name of Jesus. Amen.

ALTERNATIVE APPROACHES

◎ Divide the large group into small groups of only teens and small groups of only parents. Instruct the parents to devise a list of statements that they think teens use, and tell the teens to devise a list of statements that they think parents use.

◎ Divide the large group into family groups. Invite the families to discuss and list the statements that they hear in their own family. Then have the families rank their statements from 1 to 5, with 1 being the most important statement used in their family. For example, they might state that the most important statement used in their family is "I love you," and the second most important statement is "I am sorry." Invite the families to list the five most positive statements that they hope to use in the next week in their home.

◎ Have each small group prepare to role-play or present a skit on one or more of the situations that illustrate the use of the statements. For example, have a young person role-play asking his or her parent for money for shopping, and have an adult role-play how the parent responds. Invite them to present this before the whole group.

SCRIPTURAL CONNECTIONS

◎ Prov. 20:6–8 (Parents who have integrity have happy children.)
◎ Sir. 7:27–28 (Remember your parents with respect.)
◎ Luke 2:48–52 (Mary kept all to herself, loving her child, but challenging him to be obedient to her and Joseph.)
◎ Eph. 4:25–26 (Do not let the sun go down on your anger.)

NOTES

Use the space below to jot notes and reminders for the next time you use this strategy.

Decisions! Decisions!

OVERVIEW

This strategy gives families an opportunity to explore how family decisions are made and how they affect each member of the family.

Suggested Time

30 to 45 minutes

Group Size

This strategy should be done in small groups of no more than six people each.

Materials Needed

- ☼ newsprint, one piece for each small group and an extra sheet for the leader
- ☼ markers, one for each small group
- ☼ masking tape
- ☼ one or two packages of small self-stick notes
- ☼ pens or pencils
- ☼ two pieces of poster board

PROCEDURE

Preparation. Label a piece of poster board, "It's not fair!" and another, "But I understand!" Post these at the front of the room. Then write the following information on a piece of newsprint and post this sheet at the front of the room:

The Situation

On Monday night as your family gathers for dinner, your dad (mom) announces that he (she) has been offered a job transfer to another state. The new job begins in one month.

◎ Make a list of all the possible decisions that could be made as a result of the offer for a new job.

◎ Discuss how each possible decision would affect each family member.

◎ Discuss how the family should handle the making of each decision.

◎ Discuss who in the family should make each decision and why.

1. When the participants arrive, divide the parents into groups of no more than six people each and divide the young people into groups of no more than six people each. Give each small group a piece of newsprint and a marker.

Read the situation from the posted newsprint. Recruit a recorder for each small group. Appoint or recruit a discussion leader for each small group. Tell the groups that they have 20 minutes to go through the discussion questions. Invite the discussion leaders to facilitate this process and tell the recorders that they are to list on the newsprint their group's answers to the questions. Tell everyone that when their group discussion is completed, they should post their newsprint at the front of the room.

2. After every group has finished, invite each group's recorder to share how his or her group dealt with the situation and answered the discussion questions.

Distribute to each person six self-stick notes and a pen or a pencil. Direct everyone's attention to the pieces of poster board that you prepared before the session, labeled "It's not fair!" and "But I understand!" Tell them that you are going to read one of the small-group responses recorded on the newsprint. For example, one decision that could be made is that the whole family will move in one month so that the dad (mom) can begin his (her) new job.

Tell the participants to quickly write on a self-stick note a spontaneous personal reaction if this decision were actually made for their family. Have them post their reaction note on the poster that they think most closely corresponds to their reaction, either "It's not fair!" or "But I understand!"

When all the self-stick notes are posted, invite the group to walk silently past the posters and to read the responses that are posted. Then have everyone sit down.

3. State in your own words how most difficult decisions have ramifications for every member of a family. Sometimes decisions are not fair to some members of the family. It is important that all family members get a chance to have their feelings heard, and it is also important that each family member try to understand why a decision might be made even if it is unfair to some family members.

Close with the following prayer or one that you compose:

Leader. In those times when hard things face our families, we pray . . .
All. Guide us, O God, as we make difficult decisions.

Leader. That we may always think of each person's needs, we pray . . .
All. Guide us, O God, as we make difficult decisions.

Leader. Help us to pray in our own lives these words of Jesus: "Your will be done!" And so we pray . . .
All. Guide us, O God, as we make difficult decisions.

Leader. Our Savior made difficult decisions and always did the will of God. May we use his life as an example for our own. We ask this in the name of Jesus, who lives and reigns with the Holy Spirit, one God, forever and ever. Amen.

ALTERNATIVE APPROACHES

◎ Gather all the young people in one group and all the parents in another group. Using the situation of a possible move because of a job transfer, tell the groups to list all the *positive* ramifications of a move. For example: The young people might state that the move could provide a way to meet new and interesting friends. Or the move to a new school would give them a chance to improve their grades because they would get a second chance at doing better in their studies. The parents might suggest that the family may have an opportunity to grow closer together because everyone will have to make new friends. Maybe the new job will afford the family more money for vacations, college, or better living conditions.

After each group has had a chance to devise a list, have each group share its list with the other group. Then state in your own words the reality that every situation can have its good side if we take the time to focus on the positive aspects of it.

◎ Instead of gathering the families for this exercise, prepare it as a handout and tell the young people to take the handout home and use it with their family.

◎ Have the family groups each stay together. Tell them to think of a situation in their life that requires a decision that affects the whole family (e.g., moving, changing jobs, or changing churches). Invite them to explore all possible decisions and how they will affect each member of the family. Have them discuss the reasons why certain decisions may have to be made. Invite all the families to sit quietly asking God's guidance. Invite them to set a time when they will actually make the decision or decisions that they have identified.

SCRIPTURAL CONNECTIONS

◎ Matt. 6:34 (Do not worry about tomorrow.)
◎ 2 Cor. 4:8–9 (Even when we do not know what to do, we do not give up hope.)
◎ 1 Pet. 5:6–7 (Give all your worries to God.)

NOTES

Use the space below to jot notes and reminders for the next time you use this strategy.

Birth Order

This strategy helps young teens and their parents to understand themselves and each other better by exploring some personality characteristics that could be common to firstborn, middle, youngest, or only children.

Suggested Time

30 to 45 minutes

Group Size

This strategy should be done with a group of at least eight people.

Materials Needed

- ☼ thin-line markers, one for each person
- ☼ paper plates, one for each person
- ☼ three pieces of newsprint and a marker
- ☼ scratch paper

PROCEDURE

Preparation. Label each of three pieces of newsprint with one of the following heads: "Section A," "Section B," and "Section C." On the paper labeled "Section A," write the following words: "feels responsible, serious minded, achievement oriented, perfectionist, reliable, conscientious, likes to please, a good leader, conservative, organized, asks questions, interested in details, cautious, careful, can size up a situation, dislikes making mistakes, motivated."

On the paper labeled "Section B," write the following words: "friendly, playful, adventuresome, unpredictable, peacemaker, mediator, good manager, independent, lots of friends, avoids conflict, loyal, a realist, good social skills, good navigator, sees both sides of things, flexible thinker, not very serious."

On the paper labeled "Section C," write the following words: "kidlike, relaxed, friendly, fun loving, charming, happy-go-lucky, perceptive, a performer, cute, attention getter, convincing, master manipulator, messy, funny, persuasive, likes the limelight, likes to be pampered."

1. When you are ready to begin, make the following comments in your own words:

> Researchers are finding that a person's birth order helps shape his or her personality and influences how he or she relates to others. For example, it is not unusual for people who are firstborn children to take charge of a project or assignment.

> The goal of this activity is to give you an opportunity to try to determine how your birth order affects your behavior or the way you most commonly relate with other people.

2. Divide the large group into small groups according to the following birth orders: oldest, middle, youngest, and only. Allow no more than six people in each small group. It does not matter if adults and teens are mixed in the small groups. If your group does not have many only children, they can be grouped with the youngest children.

Instruct the group members to take turns introducing themselves by telling their group the number of siblings in their family, how many are older or younger, with which family member they spend most of their time, and with which family member they feel the closest.

3. Distribute a paper plate and a marker to each participant. Tell the participants to write their name at the top of the front of the plate and their birth order in large letters across the middle of the front of the plate.

Display the three pieces of newsprint that you prepared before the meeting. Tell everyone to read the lists and decide which of the personality traits best describe them. Direct them to write their chosen traits on the front of their paper plate. Have them count how many they have chosen from the piece labeled, "Section A," and have them write and circle that total and that section letter on the bottom of their plate. For example, if they picked eleven traits from section A, tell them to write their total like this: 11-A. Tell them to do the same for sections B and C. For example, if they picked three traits from section B and one from section C, they would write 3-B and 1-C.

Pass out scratch paper. Ask each small group to add together its members' section A totals, section B totals, and section C totals. Invite the small groups to indicate from which section they have the highest total. For example, the oldest children group may state that it has the highest total from section A.

Invite each small group to report its results to the large group. Discuss which section was most chosen by oldest children, middle children, youngest children, and only children. Try to identify patterns.

4. Invite each small group to determine the advantages and the disadvantages of its birth order. Have everyone list three positive aspects of their birth order on the back of their paper plate.

Invite the large group to discuss implications for this information in their future dealings with other people in clubs, sports teams, youth group projects, church or school committees, or family settings.

5. Close with the following prayer or one you create spontaneously on the same theme:

Guide us, Jesus, as we learn to understand that our birth order may influence our unique role in our family. May we regard our birth order as a positive blessing rather than a negative aspect in our family relationships. Help us to understand that we are who we are because of God's will, and that there is something wonderful about us whether we are the firstborn, the middle child, the youngest, or the only child in our family. We ask this in your name. Amen.

ALTERNATIVE APPROACHES

When the participants arrive, form small groups of only teens and small groups of only adults. After completing the exercise in steps 2 and 3 above, invite the young people to describe any friends they know who have the personality traits listed and have them try to determine if those friends are the oldest child, the middle child, the youngest child, or the only child in their family. Have the adults do the same for their friends. State that sometimes we can grow in our understanding of why friends behave the way they do because of our increased understanding of how behavior is influenced by birth order, and so on.

◎ Give everyone a piece of stationery and ask them to write a letter to the family member with whom they clash the most. Invite them to express in the letter how they now understand some reasons why this person acts the way she or he does.

◎ Invite all the parents present to write a prayer for their son or daughter in which they express thanksgiving and joy. Invite them to include any fears or concerns they have. Either have them put this prayer in an envelope to place on their son's or daughter's pillow at home, or use all the prayers as a closing for this gathering.

SCRIPTURAL CONNECTIONS

◎ Ps. 139:13–18 (You knit me together in my mother's womb.)
◎ Jer. 1:5–7 (Before you were born, I knew you.)
◎ Matt. 7:1–2 (Do not judge, lest you be judged.)
◎ Rom. 12:9–12 (Love with the affection of brothers and sisters.)

NOTES

Use the space below to jot notes and reminders for the next time you use this strategy.

Back-to-Back

OVERVIEW This communication activity explores how well parents and young teens communicate with each other, so that they can name some directives for developing better verbal communication skills.

Suggested Time

30 to 40 minutes

Group Size

This strategy can be done with any size group. If the group is very large, make a sound system available.

Materials Needed

☀ copies of drawings 1 and 3 (see page 32), one for each parent
☀ lapboards, one for every two people
☀ pencils with erasers, one for each person
☀ drawing paper, two sheets for each person
☀ copies of drawings 2 and 4 (see page 32), one for each teen
☀ a piece of newsprint and a marker
☀ masking tape

PROCEDURE

Preparation. Make four sample drawings as illustrated or described below, each on a separate sheet of paper. Keep them simple, using stick figures and geometric shapes.

◎ *Drawing 1*

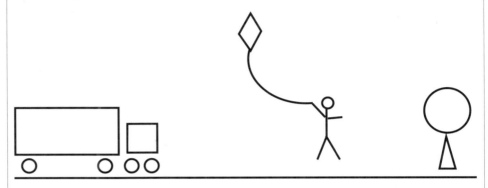

◎ *Drawing 2*

◎ *Drawing 3.* Draw a series of shapes using three rectangles, three triangles, four squares, and four circles. Draw some of them stacked on one another or arranged in a pattern. Vary the size of the shapes.

◎ *Drawing 4.* Draw a variety of balls in a consistent pattern. For example, you might draw a football, a basketball, a soccer ball, and a baseball in a row. And then you might draw another football, another basketball, another soccer ball, and another baseball continuing in that row. Use a pattern of at least two of every kind of ball. You could also draw golf balls, softballs, or tennis balls in your pattern. Make sure your drawing illustrates accurately the differences between the kinds of balls.

1. When you are ready to begin, ask the parents to pair off with their teen. Teens with more than one parent present can work with one parent at a time. Teens with no parent present may join another pair. Have the pairs sit on the floor back-to-back so that the teen cannot see the parent and the parent cannot see the teen.

Give the parents a copy of drawing 1. Give each teen a lapboard, a blank sheet of drawing paper, and a pencil with an eraser.

Tell the parents to describe their drawing to their son or daughter *without* identifying the objects in it by name. Tell the teens to draw a picture of the objects that their parent is describing. Explain to the young people that they may ask their parent to clarify any information regarding the shape or location of the objects, but they cannot ask their parent to identify the objects in the picture. Set a time limit of 5 minutes.

After 5 minutes stop the drawing and invite the pairs to compare the original picture with the teen's drawing. Invite their feedback on what made the exercise difficult.

Next, have the teens pass the lapboard and pencil to the parent, give the parents each a sheet of drawing paper, and give the teens a copy of drawing 2. Have the pairs repeat the exercise with the teens describing and the parents drawing. Again allow 5 minutes for drawing. Then have the partners compare their original and newly drawn pictures. Invite people to share their thoughts on what, if anything, made the second exercise different or easier.

Give the parents drawing 3 and the teens drawing 4, cautioning them not to show their drawing to their partner. Repeat the exercise except this time let them work together in any way they want—that is, they still cannot show the original drawing to the drawer, but they need not sit back-to-back, they may watch the drawer, they may correct the location and size of items, they may identify by name the objects to be drawn, and so on. Do not set a time limit.

2. When everyone is done, discuss what made this attempt easier. Invite them to discuss how they can apply what they have learned in this exercise to their family conversations. Brainstorm a list of five to eight skills or directives that can help parents and teenagers communicate better. List these on a piece of newsprint and post the list in the front of your room.

3. Gather the parents in a circle facing outward. Have the teens form another circle facing their parents. Have the parents and their sons or daughters hold their lapboard between them so that they are both hanging on to it. Close with the following prayer or one that you compose spontaneously on the same theme:

O God, you touched the lips of Isaiah and helped him to speak clearly so that the people would understand your commands. Help us to remember that your guidance is always available to us, too, when we are struggling to communicate better. Give us clean ears and clear vision to treat one another with love and care. We ask this in your name and in the name of Jesus, who lives and reigns with you and the Holy Spirit, one God, forever and ever. Amen.

ALTERNATIVE APPROACHES

- Instead of drawing the sample pictures, use simple drawings from a coloring book designed for very young children.
- If you have time, divide the participants into a group of parents and a group of teens. Give each group a piece of newsprint and a marker. Have the two groups gather in separate rooms. Tell the parents to list eight to ten reasons why they think it is sometimes difficult to communicate clearly with their sons or daughters. Tell the teens to list eight to ten reasons why they think it is sometimes difficult to communicate clearly with their parents. Bring the two groups back together and have each group share its list with the other. Neither group is to comment on the other's list. Tell both groups that the lists are for reflection and that they are to think about how the list is true for them. Ask everyone to make a silent pledge that they will work on their weak areas so that their family can communicate better.

SCRIPTURAL CONNECTIONS

- Matt. 13:16–17 (Blessed are your eyes and ears, for they are how you see and hear.)
- 1 Cor. 13:11–12 (Now we see indistinctly, but in the future we will see more clearly.)
- 1 Pet. 5:5–6 (Be humble with one another.)

NOTES

Use the space below to jot notes and reminders for the next time you use this strategy.

Traveling Friends Dinner

OVERVIEW

This strategy mixes several families and encourages them to get to know one another by inviting them to play games and share a meal together.

Suggested Time

60 to 180 minutes

Group Size

Each dinner party should include no more than four families.

Special Considerations

Some of the young people may want to participate, but their family may not be able or willing to. In such situations arrange to have other families "adopt" a teen for the dinner party.

Materials Needed

- ☼ notepaper, envelopes, and stamps
- ☼ a registration sheet for the traveling dinner
- ☼ a scissors
- ☼ copies of handout 1, "Traveling Dinner Activities," one for each dinner group, cut apart as scored
- ☼ supplies for creating route maps

PROCEDURE

Preparation. Select a date for the dinner and about a month ahead of time, send a note to invite all the families. Three weekends before the event, have the families who want to participate register after Masses. Make sure they include their address and phone number on the registration list.

Two weeks before the event, divide the registered families into dinner groups of three or four families each. When forming groups, try to match up people who do not know one another very well, but also group people whose homes are fairly close in order to keep travel time to a minimum.

Phone the participating families to explain which group they are in and to assign them one of the following tasks. If some groups have only three families, eliminate a task or ask someone to do two tasks:

◎ *Family 1.* Serve appetizers and be ready to lead an introductory game that will be given to you on the night of the dinner.

◎ *Family 2.* Serve either salad or soup and be ready to lead a discussion based on a handout that will be given to you on the night of the dinner.

◎ *Family 3.* Serve a main course of pasta or a casserole, and bread, and be ready to lead a sharing card game that will be explained to you on the night of the dinner. Have on hand a deck of cards for this game.

◎ *Family 4.* Serve a dessert and be ready to lead a closing prayer that will be given to you on the night of the dinner.

Create a map for each group, showing how to get to each house in the group in its assigned order. Make enough copies of each map for each family in the group.

1. On the date of the dinner, gather all the families at the church or a central place, help them gather into their assigned dinner groups, and distribute the activities from handout 1 to their respective families and give the drivers the appropriate dinner route map. You might want to encourage dinner-group members to arrange car pools.

2. Before everyone heads out for the homes of the families serving the appetizers, lead the group in the following prayer or compose one with a similar theme:

Jesus, you told us to eat and pray together in remembrance of you. You also said that wherever two or more are gathered, you are there. Bless our meals and this time together. May we be refreshed as families and may we grow to know other families in our parish more closely as we share these holy meals. In your name we pray. Amen.

ALTERNATIVE APPROACHES

◎ Instead of traveling from house to house, have all the families meet at a central place, with each family bringing its assigned part of the meal. Divide the large group into small groups of three or four families each. Try to assign families to groups with people who do not know one another very well. Give each family its assigned activity from handout 1 and have the groups do all the activities.

◎ Have all the families meet at the church before the dinner for a family eucharistic liturgy.

◎ Have all the families meet at the church or a central location after the dinner to play cards, box games, and so forth.

SCRIPTURAL CONNECTIONS

◎ Matt. 18:19–20 (Where two or three are gathered, there I am.)
◎ Mark 8:1–8 (They were hungry, and Jesus fed them.)
◎ John 15:12–15 (You are my friends if you do what I command.)
◎ Acts 4:32–34 (They held all things in common.)

NOTES

Use the space below to jot notes and reminders for the next time you use this strategy.

Traveling Dinner Activities

Make a photocopy of this handout for each dinner group. Cut apart the activities, and give each one to the families that have been assigned that task.

Introductory game. When everyone has gathered in the first home, the host family instructs all the participants to stand in a circle and introduce themselves. Each person states whether she or he is more like a fork, a knife, or a spoon, and why. After everyone has shared, then the first course is eaten.

Discussion exercise. When everyone has gathered in the second home, the host family asks all the participants to form a circle and then invites each person to answer one of the following five questions:
◎ If you are an adult, where do you work?
◎ If you are a child, where do you go to school?
◎ What does your family like to do together for fun?
◎ What is your family's favorite vacation spot?
◎ What is one of your family's favorite birthday or Christmas traditions?

Card game. This host family needs a deck of cards. Before eating, the host deals one card to each person. If the card is a heart, then the person has to state one way his or her family shows the other members of the family a sign of love. If it is a spade, then the person has to share what kind of chores or work he or she does to help out the family. If the card is a diamond, then the person names a precious possession that his or her family owns. If the card is a club, then the person shares something hard that the family has worked on together.

Closing prayer. When everyone has gathered at the home of the family serving dessert, the host family lets everyone enjoy dessert first and then leads the following prayer:

Leader. For the food that we have shared, may it nourish our bodies, we pray to our God.
All. God, hear our prayer.

Leader. For the sharing that we have enjoyed, may we continue to grow in friendship, we pray to our God.
All. God, hear our prayer.

Leader. For our parish, that it will offer food and help to poor people, we pray to our God.
All. God, hear our prayer.

Leader. In thanksgiving for the time and work that made this dinner possible, we pray to our God.
All. God, hear our prayer.

Serve Others Day

This outreach experience involves families in serving others.

Suggested Time

The time needed for this strategy varies according to the type of service the families choose.

Group Size

This strategy can be done with any size group.

Materials Needed

- ☼ notepaper, envelopes, and postage stamps
- ☼ a registration sheet for the service event
- ☼ newsprint and a marker
- ☼ a phone book or directory of service agencies
- ☼ small strips of paper, one for each family
- ☼ a pen or pencil
- ☼ a cup
- ☼ work implements for the service sites (e.g., rakes, shovels, garbage bags, construction tools, play equipment, and work gloves)
- ☼ two copies of the blessing prayer (on page 41)
- ☼ a Bible

PROCEDURE

Preparation. Two to three months before this event, organize a planning team of parents and young people. Determine a date for the Serve Others Day. Have the planning team help you contact service agencies to ask about possible service opportunities on that date. Look in your local phone book for resources. Check to see if your community has a service agency directory. The following list of agencies might give you ideas of whom to contact:

- animal shelters
- elder-care agencies
- food distribution centers
- food collection agencies
- Good Will
- Habitat for Humanity
- homeless shelters
- hospital volunteer agencies
- Meals on Wheels
- Newcomers or Welcome Wagon
- nursing homes
- the parish (ask about helping members of the parish who are homebound)
- the city parks department (ask about a park cleanup project)
- a recycling agency
- a refugee agency or a school that offers courses in English as a second language
- the Salvation Army
- soup kitchens
- thrift shops or clothing collection agencies
- a YMCA day care or day camp
- a YWCA women's shelter or child-care program

At least one month before the event, send the following note about the event to all the families:

> Are you available to gather as a family and serve others? Come to the church on _____ [insert the date] at _____ [insert the time] and be prepared to serve in one of the following agencies _____ [list the agencies]. Your service site will be a surprise, but you will work as a family. Come prepared to do anything that is needed! If you are free on our Serve Others Day, please register after Masses next Sunday.

Provide a registration sheet at all the Masses the two Sundays following the mailing of the notice.

After you get a pretty good idea of how many people are signing up for the event, meet with your planning team again. On a piece of newsprint, list the kinds of volunteer activities available at the service sites. Then determine the number of volunteers each agency can use and which projects would work best with the number of workers you have.

Then finalize arrangements with each site. Also decide how you want to conclude the workday, for example, by gathering all the families for a potluck supper or a pizza party. Notify all the participants of your plan.

The day before the event, count the number of families participating. For each family write on a slip of paper the name of a service site, based on your plans for how many people you need at each site. Mix up all the slips and place them in a cup.

1. On the day of the event, have each family randomly select a service site by drawing from the cup one of the slips of paper that you prepared. Keep parents and their sons or daughters together. Assign a team leader for each service site. Give that person any instructions and equipment that are needed to ensure that the needs of the agency are met.

2. Before everyone leaves for their site, gather all the families in a circle and recruit two readers. Have the readers join you in presenting the following prayer:

Reader 1. A reading from the Gospel of Matthew 25:34–36,40: "Inherit the kingdom prepared for you . . . for I was hungry and you gave me food, I was thirsty and you gave me something to drink."

Leader. Will those going to a soup kitchen, a food collection agency, Meals on Wheels, and any other agencies dealing with hunger and thirst please step into the circle? I ask all other people gathered here to extend their hands in blessing.

Reader 2. Bless these people, O God, as they will do your work today.

Reader 1. "I was a stranger and you welcomed me, I was naked and you gave me clothing."

Leader. Will those who will work with refugees, newcomers, homeless people, and clothing collection agencies please come forward. Let us extend our hands in blessing on these people.

Reader 2. Bless these people, O God, as they will do your work today.

Reader 1. "I was sick and you took care of me, I was in prison and you visited me."

Leader. Will all other volunteers please come into the circle? Let us extend our hands in blessing.

Reader 2. Bless these people, O God, as they do your work today.

Reader 1. When the people asked when was it they had done these things for Jesus, the Lord said, "As you did it to one of the least . . . , you did it to me."

Leader. Let us go forth now, meeting our Lord in those we serve today. Amen.

3. Remind everyone to regather at the end of the day for the concluding activity that you planned (e.g., a potluck supper or a pizza party). Then let the volunteer teams disperse to their service sites.

4. When everyone has regathered at the end of the day, divide the work groups into small groups of eight with representatives from different work groups and ask them to share their answers to the following questions:

Where did you serve? What did you do? Whom did you meet?

What did you learn about the agency with which you worked?

What is one hope you have for the people you served?

5. Conclude by reading Matt. 25:35–40.

ALTERNATIVE APPROACHES

◎ Invite one or two people in the parish to travel to the service sites and photograph the families at work. Be sure to check with the agencies where you are working to make sure this is permissible. Some agencies protect the anonymity of their clients.

◎ If you have time, gather everyone in a large group and have every person answer one of the follow-up questions from step 4. Discuss with the entire group how to organize and arrange ongoing service opportunities for families.

◎ Have the entire group work at the same site. When you gather at the end of the day, discuss some long-range activities that might change the circumstances that the service site deals with. For example, a soup kitchen might need help collecting food to serve.

◎ Invite the group to consider how to report the Serve Others Day to the rest of the parish. Recruit volunteers to report to your parish council, make a photo poster, prepare an insert for the parish bulletin, or write an article about the event for the parish newsletter or your diocesan newspaper.

◎ If the day was successful, consider making it an annual event.

NOTES

Use the space below to jot notes and reminders for the next time you use this strategy.

Love Is Heart Work

In this strategy families explore how they have behaved or can behave in ways that communicate the kind of love found in 1 Cor. 13:4–7.

Suggested Time

25 to 30 minutes

Group Size

This strategy should be done with a group no larger than thirteen families.

Materials Needed

- a Bible
- self-stick notes, thirteen for each family
- pens or pencils
- thirteen pieces of newsprint
- masking tape
- a marker
- heart stickers, one for each person

PROCEDURE

Preparation. Number thirteen pieces of newsprint from 1 to 13. Write the following phrases (paraphrased from 1 Cor. 13:4–7) on the newsprint so that the first phrase is written on the piece that is numbered 1, the second phrase is written on the piece that is numbered 2, and so on. Write in large, block letters. Then post the sheets in sequential order around your meeting space.

1. Love is patient.
2. Love is kind.
3. Love is not jealous.
4. Love does not put on airs; it is not snobbish.
5. Love is never rude.
6. Love is not self-seeking.
7. Love is not prone to anger.
8. Love does not brood over injuries.
9. Love does not rejoice in what is wrong but rejoices with the truth.
10. There is no limit to love's forbearance.
11. There is no limit to love's trust.
12. There is no limit to love's hope.
13. There is no limit to love's power to endure.

1. When the group arrives, have the participants sit on the floor in a heart-shaped arrangement. Make the following comments in your own words:

> Love is hard work, and it is heart work. Families are often engaged in heart work without realizing it. Saint Paul wrote a letter to the people of Corinth giving them a formula for heart work. That heart work is a model for family behavior.

Open the Bible to 1 Cor. 13:4–7, raise the Bible solemnly, and state, "The heart work of God!" Read the passage slowly to the group. Pause dramatically after each of the thirteen phrases.

Invite each family to form a small group. Give each family thirteen self-stick notes and a pen or pencil.

Invite everyone to look at the phrases written on the pieces of newsprint you have posted and to consider specific examples of when individuals in their family have behaved according to each phrase. Tell the families to write each example on a separate small self-stick note, along with its corresponding number. Explain that the family members should collaborate to determine their comments and that each family member should be identified at least once as a person who has displayed a behavior named in the passage.

For example, the first phrase is "Love is patient." A family might identify the mother as being consistently patient. They should write a specific example on a self-stick note, such as, "Our mother calmly keeps everyone moving when we are running late in the morning." The second phrase is "Love is kind." A family might remember that one child did all the chores when another was sick. They should write on their second note the name of the person who did the chores and a description of the behavior.

After the examples and the names of the people who represent each particular heart work are written on the self-stick notes, the family members should take turns sticking the notes to the pieces of newsprint prepared before the session. The notes should be attached to the newsprint that is labeled with the corresponding phrase. As they stick their notes on the newsprint, give them each a heart sticker to wear as a sign that they have done heart work.

When everyone has finished, read aloud to the entire group some examples from each piece of newsprint. Then invite everyone to pray, "Thank you, O God, for these heart workers!"

2. Close by having each family stand in front of a different piece of newsprint. Instruct them that you will signal them to read aloud the phrase that is on the piece of newsprint that they are standing in front of. Beginning with the first phrase, signal the group to read the phrases in sequential order. If you do not have thirteen families participating, let one or more families read more than one phrase. When the thirteenth phrase has been read, close with the following words:

Love never fails. In the end, three things last: faith, hope, and love, and the greatest of these is love.

Have each family form a circle. Tell the family to place their arms around one another's shoulders. Go up to each family group and extend your hands over them as you say the following blessing:

May the God of love bless you as you go forward to do heart work in your family. In the name of the Father, and of the Son, and of the Holy Spirit. Amen.

ALTERNATIVE APPROACHES

◎ Give each family a box of colored thin-line markers and thirteen 3-by-5-inch index cards. Tell the families each to copy onto the cards the phrases posted on newsprint around the room, putting each phrase on a separate card. Encourage them to make the phrases as colorful as possible. Tell them to take the cards home, shuffle them, and stack them upside down on their dining or kitchen table. Explain that at the next family meal, they should turn up the top card and agree that during the following week, they will do the heart work described on it. Tell them to continue to turn the cards over, one at each subsequent Sunday family meal, until all the cards have been read and the corresponding heart work has been attempted.

◎ Give to each family the following supplies: a wire hanger, a permanent marker, thirteen 24-by-1-inch pieces of ribbon, and a stapler. Direct the families each to write the phrases posted on newsprint around the room, putting each phrase on a separate piece of ribbon. Tell them to leave about 2 inches at the top of the ribbon empty. Next have them wrap the blank end of each ribbon around the bottom of their hanger and staple it closed. All thirteen pieces of ribbon should drape down from the bottom of the hanger. Tell the families to take this love banner home and hang it from a chandelier or a curtain rod in a family gathering space, such as their family room, dining room, living room, or kitchen.

◎ Assign one of the newsprint phrases to each of the families. If fewer than thirteen families are at your gathering, combine the phrases so that all thirteen are covered. Have the families devise a skit or role-play to illustrate their phrase or phrases. Explain that each skit or role-play can last only 1 minute. Have the families perform their skits or role-plays for the whole group.

SCRIPTURAL CONNECTIONS

◎ John 13:34–35 (Love one another. This is how others will know you are my disciples.)

◎ Col. 3:12–14 (Clothe yourselves with kindness, patience, and mercy.)

◎ 1 John 4:7–12 (Love is of God. If we love, God dwells in us.)

NOTES

Use the space below to jot notes and reminders for the next time you use this strategy.

Faith Connecting

OVERVIEW This faith-sharing game gives parents the opportunity to share with their children the importance of the church and faith in their own life.

Suggested Time

30 to 45 minutes

Group Size

This game should be done with no more than twelve parents and twelve teens. Each teen can have only one of his or her parents play the game. Any extra parents should become part of an audience. If you have more than twelve families, invite the extra families to be part of the audience. You might plan a second round of play that includes those extra families.

Materials Needed

- ☼ notepaper, envelopes, and stamps
- ☼ two sets of six stick-on name tags, each set numbered from 1 to 6
- ☼ one die
- ☼ twelve 10-by-10-inch pieces of poster board
- ☼ a marker
- ☼ a stopwatch, or a watch or clock with a second hand
- ☼ newsprint
- ☼ masking tape
- ☼ six copies of handout 2, "One Church, One Family"

PROCEDURE

Preparation. Send the parents a letter announcing that you will hold a Family Faith-Sharing Game Night on _____ [date and time] at _____ [location].

Make question cards by writing the following questions and directives on 10-by-10-inch pieces of poster board, one question or directive on each card:

◎ What is one reason that the church is an important part of your life?
◎ What is one of your treasured memories of growing up Catholic or of joining the Catholic church?
◎ Why are you Catholic?
◎ Why do you want your son or daughter to have a church connection?
◎ What, in your opinion, is the most important teaching of the Catholic church?
◎ Name one important person of faith who has helped you in your life.
◎ Name a Catholic hero whom you admire.
◎ Name an important teaching of Jesus by which you try to live.
◎ What is your favorite church ritual or practice?
◎ Either sing two lines of a church hymn or say two lines of a well-known prayer.
◎ What is the hardest thing about being Catholic?
◎ If you were sick and could not go to church, which church holiday or holy day would it bother you to miss?

Arrange chairs in your meeting room as diagrammed below.

□ □ □ □ □ □

□   □
□   □
□   □
□   □
□   □
□   □

□ □ □ □ □ □

There should now be six chairs in a line across each side of your room. Stack the question cards facedown in the middle of the room. Post a piece of newsprint on a wall in the room.

1. When the families arrive, divide them into two teams of six adults and six young people each. (If your group does not divide evenly into teams of six, adjust the chairs and the following procedure as needed.) Parents and their own children should be on the same team. Invite the adults on team A to sit in the set of chairs at the front of the room and have their sons and daughters sit in the

opposite set of chairs. Invite the adults on team B to sit in a set of chairs along one side of the room and invite their sons and daughters to sit in the chairs on the opposite side of the room.

2. Have the young people on team A stick on name tags that are numbered 1 to 6. Have the young people on Team B stick on another set of name tags that are numbered 1 to 6.

3. Explain that the teams will be timed, so each person should respond as quickly as possible when it is her or his turn. Roll a die. The young person on team A whose name-tag number matches the number on the die is It. It runs to the stack of cards that you placed at the center of the room, picks up the top card, and reads the question loudly. The parent of It must answer the question first. Then every adult on the team must answer the question. Time the team and record the time on the posted newsprint. The question card is placed in a discard pile.

Roll the die again. The young person on team B whose name-tag number matches the number on the die runs to the stack of cards, picks up the top card, and loudly reads the question. This person's parent must answer the question first. Then every adult on this team must answer the question. Time team B and record the time on the newsprint.

The game continues until all the questions are answered. Not every young person will get a chance to ask a question because the die will cause a random selection of Its. Declare the winner to be the team that has the shortest totaled time at the end of the game, and invite the members of that team to lead the closing prayer.

4. Ask each teen to stand beside her or his parent and have your entire group form a circle. Distribute handout 2 to the young people on the winning team. Explain that they are to share this handout with their parents and help lead the group in the closing prayer on the handout.

ALTERNATIVE APPROACHES

◎ To make the game more active and challenging, blindfold the young people and roll the die, calling out its number loudly. If a value of 5 appears when the die is rolled, then teen 5 from team A and teen 5 from team B should try to get to the stack of question cards. Explain that the parents can give verbal directions to the teens to direct them to the stack of cards. The first teen to reach the stack of cards can remove the blindfold and call out the question to his or her parent. After the first parent answers, the other parents on the team have an opportunity to answer or pass. The teen who asked the question must now sit out. The game continues until all the questions have been asked. Each team gets a point for each time every parent on the team answers the question. The total points are tallied at the end of the game. The winning team gets to lead the closing prayer.

⊚ Invite the young people to gather in a small group before the meeting and make a list of twelve questions that they would like to ask their parents about the church or faith. Have them write those questions on pieces of poster board and then play the game as described above.

⊚ Number the question cards from 2 to 12. Use a pair of dice. Provide twelve self-stick labels. Number them from 2 to 12, repeating one of the numbers so that each of the twelve labels is used, and stick at least one on each parent. Have the young people take turns rolling the dice. The parent who is wearing a number that matches the total of the dice must answer the question. That parent's son or daughter must find the question with the same number that is on the parent's label and read the question loudly. The game continues as described above.

SCRIPTURAL CONNECTIONS

⊚ Deut. 4:9–10 (Teach these things to your children and to your children's children.)

⊚ Bar. 4:21–24 (Children, do not be afraid. Your parent will call out your name to God.)

⊚ Matt. 22:24–39 (Love God with your whole heart, soul, and mind.)

NOTES

Use the space below to jot notes and reminders for the next time you use this strategy.

One Church, One Family

Leader. We gather because it is good to be a member of the Catholic family. And so let us pray to our God.

All. God, hear our prayer.

Parent 1. Let us pray for the pope, that the Holy Spirit will guide him as he leads the church into the twenty-first century.

Teen 1. May our Holy Father hear our voices so that we can become the leaders of the church as it moves into the twenty-first century. We pray to our God.

All. God, hear our prayer.

Parent 2. Let us pray for our bishop, that the Holy Spirit will guide him as he leads our diocese into the twenty-first century.

Teen 2. May our bishop hear our voices so that we can become leaders of our diocese as it moves into the twenty-first century. We pray to our God.

All. God, hear our prayer.

Parent 3. Let us pray for our pastor and pastoral staff, that the Holy Spirit will guide them as they lead our parish into the twenty-first century.

Teen 3. May our pastor and pastoral staff hear our voices so that we become leaders in our parish as it moves into the twenty-first century. We pray to our God.

All. God, hear our prayer.

Parent 4. Let us pray for the parishioners of _____ [name the parish], that the Holy Spirit will guide them as they work to be good disciples of Jesus for the twenty-first century.

Teen 4. May the parishioners of _____ [name the parish] hear our voices so that we become their leaders as we all work to be better disciples of Jesus for the twenty-first century. We pray to our God.

All. God, hear our prayer.

Parent 5. We pray too for poor, marginalized, and neglected people. Be with them, God.

Teen 5. Help us to remember that we are the workers of justice. Our voices must cry out for poor, marginalized, and neglected people. For this, let us pray to our God.

All. God, hear our prayer.

Parent 6. Let us pray for our families, that they always choose to follow the teachings of the church and learn to love the church more deeply.

Teen 6. May our families hear our voices and be with us as we grow in our love for the church. Let us pray.

All. God, hear our prayer.

A Celebration of Culture

OVERVIEW | This cultural reflection activity brings together parents and teens to explore the richness of culture and diversity.

Suggested Time

45 to 60 minutes

Group Size

This strategy can be done with a group of no more than thirty.

Materials Needed

- ☼ notepaper, envelopes, and stamps
- ☼ a small table
- ☼ four or five pairs of sunglasses (for people who forget to bring their own)
- ☼ a blanket
- ☼ several ethnic faith symbols
- ☼ a pillar candle and matches
- ☼ a Bible
- ☼ poster board, one piece for each family
- ☼ colored markers, one package for each family
- ☼ newsprint, one piece for every three families
- ☼ masking tape

PROCEDURE

Preparation. A week or two before you plan to hold this event, send families a note requesting that everyone bring a pair of sunglasses to the meeting. The note should also request that every family bring one item that represents their cultural heritage or ethnic group. List some ideas on the note. For example, one family might bring an ethnic faith symbol, another might bring a native costume. And a family with a rural heritage might bring a farm tool or seeds.

Before the families arrive, set up a small table at the front of the room. Create a faith bundle by wrapping in a blanket several ethnic faith symbols, for example, a picture of Our Lady of Guadalupe, a Celtic cross, a feather, an Asian incense burner, a small plastic bag of sage, a small plastic bag of dirt, a small plastic bag of rye, a black Madonna, and a piece of Kinte cloth. Avoid commercialized ethnic symbols like plastic colored feathers or leprechauns. Tie the items into the blanket and place it in the middle of your meeting space. Next to the bundle place a pillar candle and a Bible.

1. When the group gathers, ask the families to place their cultural symbols or objects on the small table. Recruit two readers to help with the following opening reflection:

Leader. We gather as representatives of many cultures. Our world is richer because it is inhabited by a variety of people who have interesting traditions, tasty foods, joy-filled songs, and powerful stories.

Reader 1. May we remember that we are all made in the image and likeness of God, and we are therefore precious to God and to one another.

Reader 2. From Matthew 13:47–48, we hear that the Reign of God is like a dragnet thrown into the lake, which collected all sorts of things. When it was full, the fishermen hauled it ashore, collected the things of value, and threw away what was useless.

Reader 1. We are that collection of valuable things.

Leader. May we remember to look at one another as a gift from God. We need to look beyond the unknown to see the treasures that are revealed in our diversity. [Light the pillar candle.] May this light illuminate the beauty of our cultural diversity. In God's name we pray. Amen.

Invite everyone to put on the sunglasses that they brought. Have extras on hand for people who forgot to bring a pair. Ask the following questions:

How do the sunglasses change how you see?

Does the room change, or does how you see it change?

Can you describe the difference, or is it difficult to describe?

How is cultural difference like a pair of sunglasses?

How is your reality and how you perceive all around you filtered through your culture?

Explain to the group that culture gives one roots and is often a determinant of personal identity; therefore, it is important to recognize and honor one another's cultural diversity.

Unwrap the bundle that you prepared and place the items around the edge of the blanket. Light a pillar candle. Invite the group to sit around the blanket. Lift up each item and identify by name the culture it represents and, if possible, what it symbolizes. For example:

> The Kinte cloth is an African American symbol of freedom for people whose roots can be traced back to Africa, and it is often used as a prayer cloth. [Pass the item around the circle.]

Have everyone sit with their family, and distribute to each family a piece of poster board and a package of colored markers. Explain that they are to make a poster that represents their family's cultural or ethnic heritage. Suggest that they might draw or write items such as the following:

- native costumes
- ethnic or cultural foods
- ethnic nicknames for grandparents
- culture-specific holiday or birthday traditions
- ethnic symbols
- musical instruments and faith symbols that identify their culture

2. Invite the families each to join with two other families to share their posters. Distribute a piece of newsprint to each small group and instruct the groups to make a list of five to six cultural characteristics that they can identify from the poster sharing. Have each group hang its list and share it with the large group.

3. Invite the families to walk around the small table and call each family to hold up and comment on the cultural item it brought.

4. Close by reading the following prayer or spontaneously compose one that deals with the same theme:

> Praise to you, O God, for you have created us to be reflections of your goodness. We are who we are because you have deemed it to be so. Help us always to be thankful for the richness of differences in this wonderful world you have created. Guide us to honor our own cultural roots and those of other people on this planet. We ask this in the name of Jesus, who taught us to treat one another with dignity. For he lives and reigns with you and the Holy Spirit, one God forever and ever. Amen.

ALTERNATIVE APPROACHES

◎ Hold a cultural food festival in conjunction with this strategy. Arrange for each family to bring a different ethnic potluck dish, including main dishes, breads, desserts, and pastries. Invite the families also to bring musical recordings and ethnic games like a piñata or Philippine bamboo clap sticks. Contact a folk dance teacher or a parent who could teach a folk dance so that the festival includes a time to learn an ethnic dance. Contact local ethnic restaurants for decorations and menus. Display the menus with the cultural symbols that the families brought. Invite people to find and identify the food words that are from other languages but are now common to all people, such as spaghetti, wiener, croissant, and sushi. At some point in the evening, have everyone share their findings with the whole group.

◎ Before the closing prayer, invite an immigrant or refugee family to share cultural items from their homeland and the story of their journey to this country.

◎ Instead of instructing the families to make individual posters, let everyone work together on a mural or banner. Roll out a long piece of butcher paper so that each family has a section to work on, or let the entire group work together at random. They could create a drawing of a multicultural, ethnically diverse village. Suggest that they label the banner or mural, "The City of God!"

SCRIPTURAL CONNECTIONS

◎ Gen. 1:26–27 (Humans are made in the image and likeness of God.)
◎ Rom. 12:4–7 (We, many though we are, are one body in Christ.)
◎ 1 Cor. 12:14–22 (The body is not one member; it is many.)

NOTES

Use the space below to jot notes and reminders for the next time you use this strategy.

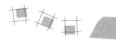

A Mother-Daughter and Father-Son Gathering About Sexuality

This gathering is designed to facilitate a serious conversation about the gift of sexuality. It gives mothers a chance to share with their daughters, and fathers a chance to share with their sons.

Suggested Time

45 to 60 minutes

Group Size

This strategy is best done with no more than thirty people.

Special Considerations

It is okay if this activity attracts only a small number of the families from your group. It is important to offer it to those who are comfortable with and willing to share about the topic of sexuality.

For this activity, every girl must have her mother or a female sponsor or guardian present. Every boy must have his father or a male sponsor or guardian present.

Materials Needed

- ☼ a Bible
- ☼ a pillar candle and matches
- ☼ newsprint and a marker
- ☼ masking tape
- ☼ stationery, one sheet for each person
- ☼ envelopes, one for each person
- ☼ pens or pencils
- ☼ a tape or CD player, and a recording of reflective music

PROCEDURE

Preparation. List the following reflection statements on a piece of newsprint and post the newsprint in your meeting room:

1. This person's favorite food, TV show, kind of music, hobby, and leisure activity are . . .

2. [Mothers complete these statements:]
   I think being a girl is special because . . .
   The most wonderful thing about you is . . .
   [Fathers complete these statements:]
   I think being a boy is special because . . .
   The most wonderful thing about you is . . .

3. When you hear the word *sex,* what do you think of? What is your definition of *sex?* What is your definition of *sexuality?*

4. This is the story of your birth. . . .

   About a month before the gathering, send all the families you wish to invite a note describing the content of the event. Instruct the parents to contact you to register or set up a registration system after church about three weeks before the gathering.

   1. Gather the parents and the young people in a circle. Open the Bible to Gen. 1:27–31. Introduce the reading with words along the following lines:

The Book of Genesis tells us a beautiful story of the creation of humans. In chapter 1 we hear: "In God's image humans were created. In the divine image God created them. Male and female God created them. God blessed them saying, 'Be fertile and multiply; fill the earth and subdue it.' God looked at every act of creation and found it to be very good" [based on vv. 27–28,31].

Light a pillar candle and read this prayer:

Creator God, you have blessed us with the gift of sexuality. May we treasure this gift and use it to draw us into a union with you and with one another. Grant that we may seek your guidance in prayer so that we learn to love others with care and respect. We ask this in Jesus' name. Amen.

2. Invite the participants to use the first reflection statement on the news-print that you posted to introduce their family member to the whole group. For example, a mother or father will introduce her or his teen by telling about the teen's favorite food, TV show, hobby, and leisure activity. Then the teen would do the same to introduce her or his parent. Go around the circle until everyone has been introduced.

3. Divide the group into family pairs so that each mother is sitting with her daughter and each father is sitting with his son. Direct the parents to share their responses to reflection statement 2 with their teen.
   Next, direct the teens to ask their parents the questions in item 3 of the newsprint list.
   Finally, invite the parents to share the story of the day of their child's birth with their daughter or son.

4. Take a short stand-up break. Distribute stationery, envelopes, and pens or pencils.

5. Invite the adults to write a letter to their child about loving. Explain that in this letter they are to describe why they feel that sexuality is a gift from God. They should also include their hopes for their child's use and discovery of the wonders of this gift. They may also share how they were introduced to sexuality as a young teenager. They should place their letter in an envelope and write their daughter's or son's name on it.
   Once the parents have started their letters, explain to the young people that their task is to write a letter to their parent listing any questions they have on the subject of sexuality. They should also include why they think their parent is special. They should place their letter in an envelope and write their parent's name on it.

6. Collect the completed letters. As a conclusion play quiet music, distribute the letters to their addressees, and invite the participants to read the letters silently.

ALTERNATIVE APPROACHES

◎ Invite both parents of each young person to attend the gathering. Both a mother and a father will accompany their daughter or son to the gathering and take part in the reflection exercise. This will increase the time needed to complete the strategy to 90 minutes. Plan a longer break with refreshments.

◎ Invite the participants to seal and address the letters. Inform the participants that you will mail the letters in a week.

◎ Instead of instructing everyone to write a letter, have the parents and teens share their reflections verbally. You will need to set a mood and provide more private space for the parents and their children. This activity would work effectively in an overnight retreat setting where parents and their daughters or sons share a sleeping room.

◎ Conduct this activity on two separate evenings, one for mothers and daughters, and one for fathers and sons.

SCRIPTURAL CONNECTIONS

◎ Gen. 2:18–24 (It is not good for man to be alone. The two of them became one body.)

◎ Matt. 19:4–6 (They are no longer two but one flesh.)

◎ John 13:34–35 (I give you a new commandment. Love one another.)

◎ 1 Cor. 13:4–7 (Love is patient.)

NOTES

Use the space below to jot notes and reminders for the next time you use this strategy.

Part B
Strategies
for Families at Home

The strategies in part B are designed for use by families at home. These strategies are intended to be photocopied and sent home to the families in your group, and so the directions in them are addressed to the parents rather than to you, the group leader. Invite the parents of the young people in your group to use or adapt the strategies to meet the needs of their family.

Options for Part B

Two of these strategies can be supplemented or adapted by you as follows.

Birthday Blessings

Instead of sending the blessing suggestions home, place one or more of the ideas in your weekly parish bulletin. Design a small corner of the bulletin to have a box or column for parents of junior high or middle school youth. Invite the parents of young teens to check that box or column for a weekly birthday suggestion and other ideas for building relationships with their teen. The twelve suggestions in this strategy could be published over an entire calendar year.

Count Your Blessings

Choose one charity for all the families to donate to and have a grand collection at the church. Organize people with vans and trucks to help transport the collection to the charity selected. Take photographic slides or make a video of the collection and distribution. Invite all families to come to a potluck dinner to view the slides or video. Make and give to each family a certificate that says something like this: "You are the hands of Christ, and because of your efforts we collected _____ light bulbs, _____ pairs of shoes, _____ sweaters, _____ coats, _____ pillows, _____ sets of glasses, and _____ blankets for the charity."

Birthday Blessings

OVERVIEW   The ideas on this handout can be used to invite God into the birthday celebrations in your home. The activities offer suggestions for a variety of birthday blessings to do in a family setting on your son's or daughter's birthday.

Suggested Time

5 to 10 minutes for each blessing activity

Group Size

Everyone in the family

Materials Needed

- ☼ colored paper
- ☼ markers
- ☼ a scissors
- ☼ glue
- ☼ a birthday cake with an extra candle, and matches
- ☼ pens and pencils
- ☼ notepaper or note cards
- ☼ a manila envelope (optional)
- ☼ a roll of butcher paper
- ☼ masking tape
- ☼ streamers or rolls of crepe paper
- ☼ balloons
- ☼ a black permanent marker

☼ a bowl of the birthday child's favorite treat
☼ small gift tags, as many as the age the birthday child is turning
☼ a box
☼ wrapping paper
☼ cellophane tape
☼ a piece of colored poster board
☼ photographs of the birthday child that you are willing to cut and paste into a collage

PROCEDURE

Encourage all the siblings to take part in the birthday blessings.

Blessing 1

Using colored paper, markers, a scissors, and glue, make a birthday card for your child. Include the words, "God's blessings on your day!" and have everyone in the family, except the birthday child of course, sign it. On the morning of your child's birthday, slip the card under his or her bedroom door.

Blessing 2

Gather the entire family to awaken the birthday person by singing "Happy Birthday." Also have each family member say, "May God bless you!" to the birthday person.

Blessing 3

Include an extra candle on the birthday cake. When that candle is lit, state, "God is with you on this special day."

Blessing 4

Work with everyone in the family to write little birthday blessing cards and hide them inside the birthday person's schoolbooks, homework, lunch bag, book bag, and so forth. Or place all the blessings in a manila envelope and place it on your daughter's or son's pillow so that she or he will find and read the blessings before going to bed.

Blessing 5

Make a special effort to take your son or daughter to school and on the way stop at the church, go inside together, and kneel for a moment of prayer thanking God for life.

Blessing 6

While your daughter or son is at school (or while another family member takes her or him away from the house for a couple of hours), decorate her or his room with birthday messages. Make a butcher paper banner that states, "God's blessings on your special day!" Hang the banner in the room. Drape streamers or crepe paper around the room. Inflate a bunch of balloons and use a black permanent marker to write on each one, "God bless your birthday!" Hang them on doorknobs, from ceiling fans, from bedposts, and so on.

Blessing 7

Prepare your son's or daughter's favorite treat, such as a bowl of popcorn, peanuts, or M&M's. On small gift tags, write, "God's blessings on your day!" Use as many gift tags as the age the child is turning. Mix these small tags into the bowl of treats and set it out for him or her.

Blessing 8

If your child's school permits deliveries to students, arrange for a florist to deliver a flower or birthday balloon to your son or daughter at school. Make sure the gift card states, "God bless you on your birthday."

Blessing 9

At the family dinner table (or at a restaurant if you go out for a birthday meal), prepare to share with the birthday child the positive feelings you and the rest of the family experienced when she or he was born. Begin each comment by saying, "On the day you were born, God smiled because _____ [fill in the blank with a family member's name and his or her response to the birth]." For example, you might say, "On the day you were born, God smiled because your dad was so proud he took a picture of everyone in the hospital, including the janitor!"

At the end of the family birthday dinner, share the story of the day of the birth of your child. Tell about all the details of who was there, how the family got to the hospital, the doctor or midwife's name and actions. Include any humorous or touching events. Share the excitement you felt and the hopes and dreams that you had for him or her.

Blessing 10

Ask the birthday girl or boy to compose and share with the family a prayer of thanksgiving to God for her or his life.

Blessing 11

Write a note that says, "God thinks you are special, and so do we!" Place it in a box and wrap the box. When it is time for the birthday person to open gifts, have him or her open the message box first. Then invite each member of the family to trace the sign of the cross on the forehead of the birthday boy or girl and to state as they do so, "God bless you!"

Blessing 12

Write "Blessed!" in large block letters on a piece of colored poster board. Collect photographs of your daughter or son from her or his birth until the present. Cut the photographs so that they fit into the letters of the word "blessed." Glue or tape them into the letters. Overlap and cluster them so that they make a collage. Present the poster to your daughter or son as a birthday gift.

SCRIPTURAL CONNECTIONS

◎ Gen. 12:2–3 (God will bless you and make your name great.)
◎ Deut. 7:13–14 (You will be blessed among all people.)
◎ Ps. 118:23–24 (This is the day the Lord has made; let us rejoice and be glad!)

NOTES

Use the space below to jot notes and reminders for the next time you use this strategy.

Count Your Blessings

OVERVIEW   Read the following activities and consider using them with your family over the next few weeks to learn about helping others. If you choose to use these ideas, as a family each week you will do a 10- to 15-minute activity that focuses on the needs of others. During these activities you are going to collect household items for poor people, you are going to tax yourselves a certain monetary value for any excessive usage of luxuries, and you are going to share your possessions with others.

    This strategy can be used anytime, but it might be especially effective during Advent or Lent.

Suggested Time

10 to 15 minutes for each of six weekly components

Group Size

Everyone in the family

Materials Needed

- ☼ a phone book or local social-services directory
- ☼ a collection receptacle such as a jar or an envelope or a bank
- ☼ a marker
- ☼ a piece of poster board
- ☼ a big box
- ☼ two new pillowcases (optional)

PROCEDURE

Preparation. Look in the phone book or in a social-services directory for a charity such as the Salvation Army, Goodwill, the Red Cross, or a local shelter. As a family select a charity for your gifts.

Divide a piece of poster board into six sections, number the sections 1 to 6, and label each section with a different one of the following headings:

◎ Light up the world
◎ Walk the walk
◎ Clothe the naked
◎ Rest your weary head
◎ For you were thirsty
◎ May God's love warm you

Place a big box in a central place in your home for the material possessions that you will be sharing. Label the box, "Sharing box," and set the poster you created beside it. In the middle of your dining room table, place a collection receptacle of some sort for use as a bank.

Week 1: Light Up the World

Just before dinner one night this week, have everyone in the family count the number of lightbulbs you have burning. Determine a tax you will pay on each light that is on. Collect the money and place it in the bank that you have set out for this purpose. For example, if your family decided to pay a tax of five cents for each burning lightbulb and eleven lights are on, put fifty-five cents in the bank. The gift for this week is lightbulbs. Put a package of lightbulbs in the sharing box that you prepared.

Week 2: Walk the Walk

Have everyone count how many pairs of shoes your family owns and charge yourselves a tax for each pair. Place that money in your bank. Collect any pairs of good shoes or shoes people have outgrown that you do not wear or are willing to give away and put them in your sharing box. Explain to your family that sharing is and should be a sacrifice. They should not expect to go shopping to buy something new to replace what they have given away. Explain that this strategy can help the family to simplify their life and to divest themselves of some of their abundance.

Week 3: Clothe the Naked

Count all the sweaters and coats your family owns. Determine the tax you will pay on each one, collect the money, and place it in your bank. Have everyone in the family select one of their good sweaters or coats and place it in the sharing box.

Week 4: Rest Your Weary Head

Have the family members go around the house and count all the pillows they find, even decorative pillows and those stored in closets. As a family determine a tax for each pillow and place the appropriate money in your bank. Place two pillows in the sharing box. If possible also include a gift of two new pillowcases.

Week 5: For You Were Thirsty

Gather the family in the kitchen and count the drinking glasses there. Then check other places in your home where drinking glasses may be stored or used, such as the china cupboard or the bathroom. Determine a tax for each glass and place the appropriate amount in your bank. Find six nice matching glasses and place them in the sharing box.

Week 6: May God's Love Warm You

Have your family count the blankets in your house, including afghans or coverlets. Determine a tax for each and place that money in your bank. Find a good blanket or coverlet and place it in the sharing box.

As a family choose a time to deliver your box and money to the charity, shelter, or collection agency that you have chosen.

Dedication of the Gifts

Before you deliver the money and the items you have collected, gather as a family around the sharing box. Place your bank in or near the sharing box. Divide and share the reading of the following adaptation of Isa. 58:3,6–9:

The people cried out to God, "Should we fast and make sacrifices even when you do not notice it?" God replied, "This, rather, is the fasting I wish: releasing those bound unjustly, untying the thongs of the yoke; setting free the oppressed and sheltering the homeless, clothing the naked when you see them, and not turning your back on your own.

"Then your light shall break forth like the dawn. The glory of God shall be your rear guard. Then you shall call and our God will answer, you shall cry for help and God will say: 'Here I am.'"

ALTERNATIVE APPROACHES

◎ Feel free to decide on different items to be counted and collected. Make it a family decision—discuss with everyone what they would like to collect and how they would like to sacrifice. You may decide to do something with food. For example, you might collect food for a pantry, a shelter, or a soup kitchen. You may decide to save money by sacrificing and then use the money to buy menu items for a meal that you make, deliver to, and serve at a soup kitchen.

- Invite other families who are participating in this strategy to challenge their friends and relatives to also join in, pooling everyone's money and donations. Then challenge everyone to see who can gather the most money and items.
- Plan a special culminating activity for week 6. For example, share in a special meal with other families who did this activity, or serve food as a family at a community meal program or homeless shelter.

SCRIPTURAL CONNECTIONS

- Ps. 34:6,18 (God hears the cry of poor people.)
- Prov. 31:8–9 (Speak for those who cannot speak for themselves.)
- Matt. 5:3,6 (Blessed are the poor. Blessed are those who hunger and thirst for justice.)

NOTES

Use the space below to jot notes and reminders for the next time you use this strategy.

Prayers of Fire and Water

OVERVIEW

This at-home prayer activity gives your family members a chance to pray for many needs and to bless one another.

Suggested Time

3 to 5 minutes for each person

Group Size

Everyone in the family

Materials Needed

- a Bible
- a candle and wooden matches
- a coffee can half filled with water
- 2-by-3-inch strips of paper, one for each person
- pens or pencils
- a small basket
- a small, clear bowl of water

PROCEDURE

Preparation. Place the following items on the kitchen or dining room table: a coffee can half full of water, a Bible, a candle, wooden matches, 2-by-3-inch strips of paper (one for each family member), and pens or pencils. Place a small, clear bowl of water and a small basket in the middle of the floor in another room.

1. Gather your family around the dining room or kitchen table. Read Eph. 6:18 from a Bible.

2. Light a candle and explain that each person should, in turn, light a wooden match from the candle and hold it over a coffee can half filled with water. Tell them that as the match burns, the person holding the match is to name as many needs or give thanks for as many blessings as he or she can think of. Explain to everyone that when the flame gets close to their fingers, they are to blow out the match and put it in the can of water. The match serves as a timer for each individual's prayer.

Give each person a match. Have the youngest person light her or his match by holding it to the candle flame. Invite that person to pray for needs in the family and the world and to give thanks for what is good in her or his life. Encourage the speaker to keep praying until the flame is close to the end of the match. When this person douses the match, pray as follows:

Leader. "For these many needs and for the blessings of _____ [name the person], we beg for your help and offer thanks, O God, as we pray . . ."

All. God, hear us.

Continue in this fashion until everyone has had a turn.

3. Read Isa. 43:1–3 from the Bible. Then instruct everyone to take one of the strips of paper that you set out and write on it one fear they have for their family. The fear can be for a particular family member or for the entire family. After they have written their fear, direct them to hold the paper and go to the room where you have set out a bowl of water and a small basket. Bring the Bible with you. When everyone has entered this room, invite the family to stand in a circle around the bowl of water.

Go to the inside of the circle, pick up the bowl and the basket, and stand in front of one of the family members. Tell him or her to place his or her strip of paper in the basket and to take the basket. Dip your hand in the water and trace the sign of the cross on that person's forehead, saying: "Do not be afraid. God is with you."

Move to the next person with the bowl and the basket and bless him or her in the same way. Continue blessing everyone in the circle. Then let the last person you bless do the same for you. Place the basket by the Bible and close the experience by reading Isa. 43:4–5.

ALTERNATIVE APPROACHES

- ◎ Use the match-prayer part of this strategy as a birthday prayer. Place a long wooden fireplace match on the family member's birthday cake. Light the match. Invite every member of the family to share a prayer for the birthday person. When the match burns out, the prayer is complete.
- ◎ Use long fireplace matches instead of the small wooden ones. Use only one, and when it is lighted, each person in the family must state a one-sentence prayer request or a few words of praise. The family members keep taking turns adding sentences to the prayer until the match burns out. When the match burns out, the prayer is complete.
- ◎ Place the strips of paper on which the family members wrote their fears in a fireplace or an outdoor grill and burn them. As the strips of paper burn, invite the family to join hands and to pray the Lord's Prayer together.

SCRIPTURAL CONNECTIONS

- ◎ Isa. 41:8–10 (Be not dismayed, for God will strengthen you and help you. Fear not, God is with you.)
- ◎ Deut. 31:7–8 (God goes before you, so do not be dismayed. God will never fail you, so do not fear.)
- ◎ Phil. 4:4–7 (Present your needs to God in every form of prayer.)

NOTES

Use the space below to jot notes and reminders for the next time you use this strategy.

Suits You

OVERVIEW

The activity on this handout can be used to help the members of your family communicate better. It gives everyone a chance to learn what they value and appreciate about one another.

Suggested Time

20 to 30 minutes

Group Size

Everyone in the family

Materials Needed

☼ a deck of cards

PROCEDURE

Preparation. Separate a deck of cards into four stacks by suit.

Designate one member of the family as the dealer. The dealer distributes the cards so that each person receives four cards, one card from each suit. Have the family members stack their four cards in front of them. Explain that every suit is a symbol for a theme of conversation.

Start with the oldest member of the family, instructing him or her to turn over the top card in his or her stack.

If the card that is turned over is a heart, the dealer says, "Love." The player has to either name one person in the family who recently has shown him or her love or name something he or she loves about the family.

If the card that is turned over is a spade, the dealer says, "Work." The player has to either name some work that the family needs to have done around the house to make life easier on the rest of the family or describe some kind of work that she or he will be involved in to help the family. For example, a teen might state that she or he needs to work in the family garden.

If the card that is turned over is a diamond, the dealer says, "Precious or special!" The player has to either name a precious thing that the family possesses or name a family activity that is special to him or her.

If the card that is turned over is a club, the dealer says, "Tough stuff!" The player has to either name something that is hard or difficult in family life or something tough that the family will be dealing with in the future.

After the oldest player has turned over his or her first card and completed the task, the next person sitting clockwise turns over his or her top card and completes the task.

The play continues until everyone has turned over all their cards and finished their tasks.

ALTERNATIVE APPROACHES

◉ Deal the cards at random so that each person has four cards not necessarily from different suits. The player must respond to the conversation-starter symbol of each card even though he or she might have all hearts, or two diamonds and two spades, and so forth. The player must think of different responses even though the responses deal with the same topic.

◉ Change the game so that if a person gets a face card, she or he must respond as follows:

King. If a king is turned over, the player is declared to be Ruler of the Universe and must share what he or she would do to make the world a better place for all people.

Queen. If a queen is turned over, the player is declared Ambassador to the Poor and must share what he or she would do to help poor people in your state.

Jack. If a jack is turned over, the player is declared Jack-of-All-Trades and must share how he or she would make sure all people had a home to live in.

Joker. If a joker is turned over, the player can skip his or her turn, but first must designate a suit for the joker and pick someone to respond accordingly.

◎ Invite another family to play a similar game with your family. Divide into teams so that players from both families are on both teams. Play any common children's card game like Go Fish or War. Whoever wins the hand is the person who gets to do the conversation. For example, if the game is War and the person who won the hand wins it with a ten of hearts, then she or he has to state who in her or his family has shown her or him love recently and how.

SCRIPTURAL CONNECTIONS

◎ Ps. 143:10–12 (Teach us to do your will and free us from distress.)
◎ John 6:28–29 (Having faith in Jesus is doing the work of God.)
◎ 1 Thess. 3:11–13 (May your love for one another overflow.)
◎ 1 Pet. 1:6–9 (Your faith is more precious than gold.)

NOTES

Use the space below to jot notes and reminders for the next time you use this strategy.

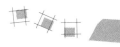

Post Your Beliefs

OVERVIEW

This at-home family activity gives family members a chance to state their individual beliefs in writing, to share those beliefs with one another, and to affirm one another.

Suggested Time

About 45 minutes

Group Size

Everyone in the family

Materials Needed

- ☼ copies of handout 3, "The Apostles' Creed"
- ☼ a scissors
- ☼ pens or pencils
- ☼ notebook paper, one sheet for each person
- ☼ packets of self-stick notes

PROCEDURE

1. Gather your family and, using copies of handout 3, pray the Apostles' Creed together. Remind your family that it is different from the Nicene Creed, which they may be accustomed to hearing as it is often recited at Mass.

Count the number of family members who are taking part in this strategy. Cut apart one copy of the creed so that each family member gets a sentence or more. For example, one piece might include the first three sentences, which begin "I believe in God," "I believe in Jesus," and "He was born." Distribute pens or pencils and tell everyone to write their name on the back of their piece of the creed.

2. Then have everyone trade pieces of paper. Instruct everyone to compose a prayer on the back of their piece of the creed for the person whose name is on their paper. The prayer must include an "I believe" statement and some thought that refers to the piece of the creed that appears on the other side of the paper. For example, the first piece of the creed might have a prayer such as the following:

> Mom, I believe that you are one of the most special parts of the Creator's work. I pray that Jesus and Mary will watch over you this week. Amen.

Share the creed prayers with one another and then have the prayer composers give their prayer to the person it was written for.

3. Distribute notebook paper to everyone and tell them to write across the top of their paper, "My beliefs." Then direct them to list the numbers 1 to 10 down the left margin of their paper. Read the following statements and have the participants complete them by writing one response beside each number:

1. In regard to God, I believe . . .

2. In regard to Jesus, I believe . . .

3. In regard to the church, I believe . . .

4. In regard to education, I believe . . .

5. In regard to poor people, I believe . . .

6. In regard to death, I believe . . .

7. In regard to drugs or alcohol use, I believe that God . . .

8. In regard to sexuality, I believe that God . . .

9. In regard to prayer, I believe . . .

10. In regard to my family, I believe . . .

Take time for the family members to share their responses with the rest of the family.

4. Distribute self-stick notes so that everyone has enough to write separate messages to everyone else in the family. The messages should use the following

pattern: "_____ [insert name], I believe that you . . . and I pray that God will . . ." Tell them to include a prayer of affirmation.

Explain that everyone should hide their "I believe . . ." messages so that family members will find the ones meant for them at unexpected moments in unexpected places. For example, a note written to a sister might be placed on the bathroom mirror so that she sees it when she gets up in the morning. Tell everyone to hide the notes before going to bed for the night.

5. To conclude, invite everyone to join hands. Designate one person to pray silently for the person on her or his right and tell that person to gently squeeze the hand of the person on the right to indicate when she or he is finished. The person whose hand was just squeezed then prays silently for the person to his or her right and gently squeezes that person's hand when the prayer is finished. This continues until everyone in the circle has had a chance to pray and has had someone pray for them.

ALTERNATIVE APPROACHES

◎ Hold a contest to see who is the most creative in hiding the messages. The messages can be placed anywhere that is not dangerous or impossible to find. Some good places are in briefcases, in book bags, and on the steering wheel of the car.

◎ Do this activity on a family vacation. Make sure everyone understands the process before you begin. Have one person deliver a prayer to someone else without telling the recipient who the sender was. The recipient secretly hides it for one of the other family members. The game continues until all the family members have had the prayer. The family members should get as creative as possible when it is their turn to hide it.

◎ Assign a special day for one family member and make that person the only recipient of the self-stick messages; for example, on a birthday, a wedding anniversary, or a graduation day.

SCRIPTURAL CONNECTIONS

◎ Matt. 13:44–46 (Our beliefs are so precious that they are like a treasure hidden in a field.)

◎ Luke 22:19–20 (Jesus told us to break bread in remembrance of him.)

◎ John 20:11–18,29 (Jesus rose from the dead, and we believe without seeing.)

NOTES

Use the space below to jot notes and reminders for the next time you use this strategy.

The Apostles' Creed

I believe in God,
    the Father almighty,
    creator of heaven and earth.
I believe in Jesus Christ,
    his only Son, our Lord.
He was conceived by the power of the Holy
      Spirit and born of the Virgin Mary.
He suffered under Pontius Pilate,
    was crucified, died, and was buried.
    He descended into hell.
On the third day he rose again.
He ascended into heaven and is seated at the
      right hand of the Father.
    He will come again to judge the living and
    the dead.
I believe in the Holy Spirit,
    the holy catholic Church,
    the communion of saints,
    the forgiveness of sins,
    the resurrection of the body,
    and the life everlasting,
    Amen.

(Catechism of the Catholic Church,
pages 49–50)

      Handout 3: Permission to reproduce this handout for program use is granted.

Photo Gallery

Enjoy a special time together recalling the sacramental moments in your family's history. This at-home activity uses a game and your photo collection as a discussion-starter.

Suggested Time

60 to 120 minutes

Group Size

Everyone in the family

Materials Needed

- ☼ a coffee table, other low table, or blanket
- ☼ a bowl of water
- ☼ Band-Aids, one for each person
- ☼ two pieces of bread on a plate
- ☼ a small saucer of baby oil or lotion
- ☼ a medicine bottle (if applicable)
- ☼ a stole and chalice (if applicable)
- ☼ a wedding ring
- ☼ notebook paper
- ☼ a pen or pencil
- ☼ a thin-line marker
- ☼ a basket
- ☼ a collection of photographs of the family's sacramental moments

PROCEDURE

Preparation. Find family photos of sacramental moments and group them by sacrament. That is, stack all the Baptism photos together, all the first Communion photos together, and so on.

Put a coffee table, some other type of low table, or a blanket in the middle of the living room. Place the following items on the table or blanket: a bowl of water, Band-Aids, a plate with two pieces of bread on it, a saucer of lotion or oil, a medicine bottle (if applicable), a stole and chalice (if applicable), and a wedding ring.

Write one of each of the following numbered items on seven index cards and place these index cards facedown in a basket:

Baptism: godparents, church, name, water
Reconciliation: confession, forgiveness, secrecy
Communion: body, blood, host, chalice, eating
Confirmation: Holy Spirit, commitment, gifts, sponsor, oil
Marriage: vows, bride, groom, rings
Anointing: sick, oil, hands, hospital
Holy Orders: stole, chalice, vows

1. Gather the family members around the coffee table, other low table, or blanket that you prepared. Tell them that they are going to play a game and take a memory trip through your family's sacramental history. Explain that the bowl of water, the Band-Aids, the bread, the oil, the medicine bottle (if applicable), the stole and chalice (if applicable), and the ring are all symbols of sacraments that family members have experienced. Explain that everyone will draw an index card out of the basket. Tell them that the card will have on it the name of a sacrament and a word list. Their task is to describe the sacrament to the rest of the family without using the name of the sacrament or any of the words on the list. The object is to get the other family members to guess which sacrament is being described. For example, if they choose a paper that has "Anointing: sick, oil, hands, hospital" on it, they must use other words as clues to describe the sacrament. An example is, "A priest gathers with a family before surgery and prays with the family for healing and comfort."

2. Select one person to begin the game. Tell that person to draw a piece of paper from the basket and to describe the sacrament that is named on the piece of paper. Once the sacrament is identified, ask the following questions:

- Who remembers the celebration of this sacrament for _____ [name one of the family members]?

- Who was there? What was the name of the priest involved?

- Did anything unusual happen? How did this celebration help us feel closer to one another? to God?

From the photograph collection that you prepared, bring forward those of that particular sacrament. Have the family go through them and spend time sharing memories and asking questions about who is in the photographs, details of what the celebration was like, and so forth.

Before moving on to the next sacrament, do the corresponding ritual from the following list:

◎ *Baptism.* Take a bowl of water, face the person next to you, touch the water in the bowl, and touch the forehead of the person facing you, stating, "May this water remind you that you are a child of God." The person who was just blessed takes the bowl and repeats the action and words with the person next to her or him. This ritual continues until every member of the family is blessed with water.

◎ *Reconciliation.* Remind everyone that the sacrament of Reconciliation is a sacrament of healing. Place a Band-Aid on the back of each person's hand. Turn to the person next to you and, with a thin-line marker, write, "You are forgiven," on his or her Band-Aid. Pass the marker to that person so that he or she can do the same for the person next to him or her. This ritual continues until everyone's Band-Aid has been written on.

◎ *Eucharist.* Invite everyone to think of a need in the world, in the community, or in the family. Break some bread into enough pieces for everyone and for use in the closing prayer. Pass a plate of the bread pieces around the family and instruct everyone to take a piece of bread and hold it. When everyone has a piece of bread, have them eat silently while praying for the need they identified.

◎ *Confirmation.* Dip your thumb into a saucer of lotion or oil. Trace the sign of the cross on the palms of the person next to you while stating, "Use your gifts for others!" Have that person do the same action and say the same words to the next person. This ritual continues until everyone has blessed another family member and has been blessed. Invite everyone to rub their palms together until the lotion or oil is absorbed.

◎ *Anointing of the Sick.* If someone in the family has experienced the sacrament of Anointing of the Sick, pass the medicine bottle and have each person compose and state a prayer-sentence for any family member or friend who is sick.

◎ *Holy Orders.* If someone in the family has experienced the sacrament of Holy Orders, pass around the stole and chalice and have each person name one way they can each be a priest or servant or helper for others.

◎ *Marriage.* Hold up the wedding ring and state: "This ring symbolizes our family's joys and difficulties. It is a sign of the commitment of this couple in this family. As the ring is passed, name a positive characteristic of this couple's marriage." Pass the ring as each person affirms the couple.

3. Select another person to draw a sacrament from the basket, and repeat procedure step 2 for that sacrament. Continue in this manner until all the sacraments have been explored.

4. End the evening with prayer. Have the family stand in a circle and let family members hold the sacramental symbols. Pray:

> We are a sacramental people. God touches us through water and oil, through healing, through bread, and through relationships. May we continue to journey as sacraments of God by _____. [Invite each person to name one way he or she will reach out to others. The following is a list of possible responses: collecting food for the hungry, doing chores without being asked, forgiving my friend.]

ALTERNATIVE APPROACHES

- ◎ Designate a wall in the home for a sacramental display and hang the photographs of as many sacramental moments as possible on that wall.
- ◎ Buy a large poster frame for each family member and set aside one evening to make sacramental collages. Each married couple or person takes all the photographs of his or her sacramental moments and puts them into a collage. Invite the family members to hang the finished collages on one wall in the home or let everyone hang their collage in their own room.
- ◎ You might need several gatherings to do all the sharing called for in this activity. You could focus on a different person at each session, or you could focus on a different sacrament each time.

SCRIPTURAL CONNECTIONS

- ◎ Matt. 3:13–17 (Jesus is baptized in the Jordan River.)
- ◎ Matt. 19:4–6 (Jesus teaches us about the covenant of marriage.)
- ◎ Mark 14:22–26 (the story of the Last Supper)
- ◎ Luke 7:36–50 (Jesus forgives the penitent woman.)
- ◎ John 20:19–23 (Jesus breathes the Holy Spirit into the disciples.)
- ◎ Heb. 5:1–6 (Jesus is the high priest.)
- ◎ James 5:14–15 (Anoint and pray for those who are sick.)

NOTES

Use the space below to jot notes and reminders for the next time you use this strategy.

Sharing Tough Times

This activity gives family members a chance to share a conversation about the tough times they have faced in the past and how they have faced those difficulties and moved on in their life.

Suggested Time

30 to 45 minutes

Group Size

Everyone in the family

Materials Needed

- ☀ a candle and matches
- ☀ three 3-by-5-inch cards
- ☀ a marker
- ☀ a box of tissues
- ☀ cellophane tape
- ☀ a checkbook
- ☀ a Bible
- ☀ pebbles, one for each person

PROCEDURE

Preparation. Label each of three 3-by-5-inch cards with a different one of the following words: "Death," "Broken," and "Security."

Place a candle in the middle of your dining room or kitchen table and surround the candle with pebbles, at least as many as the number of people participating in this activity. Place around the candle a box of tissues, a roll of cellophane tape, and a checkbook. Also set out a Bible and matches.

1. Open the meeting by lighting a candle and praying the following prayer or one you compose spontaneously on the same theme:

 O God, you are our God, and we will ever sing your praises. Be with us as we face our tough times. May this light be a constant reminder that you promised always to be with us, in our good times and especially in our bad times. With confidence and trust, we place our needs in your hands. Amen.

As everyone else sits silently, hold up the card you prepared that is labeled "Death" and place it by a box of tissues. Then hold up the card labeled "Broken" and place it by a roll of cellophane tape. Hold up the card labeled "Security" and place it by the checkbook.

2. Explain that this time together will be focused on the tough times that your family has faced or will face, either as individuals or as a family unit. Explain in your own words that Jesus also faced tough times in his life and that he always turned to God for comfort. God did not change the situation, but Jesus knew that God was with him even in the most painful times.
Read John 11:1–3,32–34.

3. Hold up the card labeled "Death" and ask the following questions:

 What experiences of death have we had as a family?

What or who helped you to deal with that death?

What is scary or difficult about dealing with death?

After each question ask for a volunteer to take a turn sharing. Pass him or her the tissue box to hold while speaking. If someone does not want to share, they may pass the box of tissues to the next person. When everyone has had a turn, the entire family holds hands and prays, "God be with us in our tough times!"
Read Matt. 26:36–40.

4. Hold up the card labeled "Broken" and ask the following questions. This time as each person shares, she or he should hold the roll of tape.

 "What experiences of being broken or rejected have we had as a family or as individuals?

Think of a friendship or relationship that broke apart. What or who helped you deal with that experience of being broken or rejected?

What is scary or difficult about dealing with being broken or rejected?

When everyone has had a turn, the entire family holds hands and prays, "God be with us in our tough times!"
Read Matt. 6:31–34.

5. Hold up the card labeled "Security." Explain that feelings of insecurity can be caused by a financial situation, a lack of some possession, a loss of self-confidence, or the prospect or reality of difficulty at a job. Continue with the following questions. As each person shares, she or he should hold the checkbook.

What experiences have we had where we have felt insecure?

What or who helped you deal with this issue of security?

What is scary or difficult about dealing with issues of security?

When everyone has had an opportunity to share, the family joins hands and prays, "God be with us in our tough times!"

6. Give each person one of the pebbles that you placed around the candle as a symbol of family unity. Explain the symbol with words along the following lines:

A pebble is a mountain seed. Mountains cannot be broken or moved. A mountain forms a secure boundary around its valleys and neighboring towns. A mountain stands firm even in adverse times of storms, floods, and so forth. The pebbles are a reminder that everyone in the family supports everyone else, especially during tough times. I invite you always to carry your pebble in a purse or a pocket as a symbol of your family's support.

ALTERNATIVE APPROACHES

◎ This strategy could be done over several sessions. Consider covering one topic a night once a week. This format will give each person plenty of time for individual sharing.

◎ On each 3-by-5-inch card that identifies the tough time, write the specific experience or experiences that the family members describe. Attach the cards to the refrigerator so that everyone remembers to pray for one another whenever they see the cards.

◎ Identify and discuss other tough time issues that affect your family life. Think of a common household object that symbolizes each issue and use it for your conversation.

◎ Establish a prayer space in your home, such as a small table with a Bible and a candle. On this table collect objects that symbolize tough times in your family's life. Every month gather the family and pray together for guidance from God and to help support one another as you struggle with the pain of tough times.

SCRIPTURAL CONNECTIONS

◎ Isa. 53:1–4 (God is revealed to those who are spurned and rejected and not held in high esteem by others.)
◎ Matt. 6:25–28 (Look at the birds in the sky and flowers in the fields. God gives them what they need.)
◎ Luke 12:22–29 (Stop worrying about material things; you are more important to God than ravens and lilies, and God takes care of them.)
◎ 1 Pet. 2:19–21 (Follow the example of Christ and look for the grace that comes when one experiences sorrow and suffering.)

NOTES

Use the space below to jot notes and reminders for the next time you use this strategy.

Part C
Strategies
for Teen Groups or Classes

The following strategies are designed for gatherings of young teens. Invite the young people in your group to meet at the same place and time to enjoy the activities together. The strategies are designed to be used in religious education classes, youth ministry programs, retreats, or any place young teens gather to examine issues that affect them and their relationships with themselves, with their families, and with God.

Table Fable

OVERVIEW

This activity is designed to help the young people reflect on how decisions are made in their family and what factors contribute to the dynamics of the decision-making process.

Suggested Time

10 to 15 minutes

Group Size

No more than ten people

Materials Needed

- unlined white paper, one sheet for each person
- pens or pencils
- red crayons or markers, one for each person
- blue crayons or markers, one for each person
- newsprint and a marker
- masking tape
- 3-by-5-inch cards, one for each person
- a Bible

PROCEDURE

Preparation. Write the following questions on a piece of newsprint and post it at the front of your room:

◎ Should everyone in the family be included in making a decision concerning the family? Why or why not?

◎ What decisions, if any, should everyone in the family be included in?

◎ Does your family's table seating arrangements reveal anything about the leadership style in your family? If so, what?

1. Give each person a piece of unlined white paper, a pen or pencil, a red crayon or marker, and a blue crayon or marker. Invite the young people to draw a picture of the table where most of their family eats most of its meals.

Then have them draw the seating arrangement that is typical for their family and put the names of their family members by their usual seats. For example, if their father sits at the head of the table, they should write his name over the chair that is at the head of the table. Or, if they have a round table, they should note who generally sits next to whom.

Then have them draw a red circle around the name of each person who makes important decisions in the family and a blue circle around the name of each family member, if any, who makes no decisions in the family.

2. Divide the participants into groups of three or four people each. Explain the small-group process as follows:

In your small groups, each of you will have an opportunity to share your table drawing and explain its seating arrangement. Let the person whose birthday is closest to today's date go first. Then proceed around the group clockwise. Also address the following points:

Tell about a specific family decision, such as how your family decided who does which chores.

Do you think you should have more say in family decisions? If so, why?

After they have finished sharing, invite the small groups to discuss the questions on the newsprint that you posted before the session.

3. Distribute a 3-by-5-inch card to everyone. Have them write the following on their card:

I honor my parents' right to make decisions, and I think I have the right to be consulted on the following issues:

Invite the young people to think of areas of family decision making that they would like to have some input on. Have them list those on their card.

Give them the option of taking the card home and using it as a conversation-starter with their parents or leaving the card in the group Bible and praying for guidance from God.

Open the Bible and allow those who want to place their card in the Bible to do so. Then read Ps. 119:1–5.

ALTERNATIVE APPROACHES

◎ Have the small groups each devise a skit or role-play that takes place at a family dinner. Explain that the skit or role-play should include the seating arrangement at the family table and illustrate who usually makes the decisions. Tell the groups that their performance should be realistic and include an issue that involves a decision.

After each group does its skit or role-play, lead the large group in a discussion of the following questions:

Did the family members in the skit or role-play include everyone in the decision?

How could they have included everyone?

What are some ways that teenagers can get their parents to include them in decisions that affect them?

◎ Invite the young people to paint or draw a picture of their family's meal table. Have them label their picture with a song title that reminds them of their family's way of making decisions. For example, "The Battle Hymn of the Republic" might be a reference for a family that argues about most of its decisions, and "Hush, Hush, Somebody's Calling My Name" might be a reference for a family that includes everyone in its decision making.

SCRIPTURAL CONNECTIONS

◎ Exod. 20:12 (Honor your father and mother.)
◎ Deut. 6:20–25 (Parents should teach the statutes of the Lord.)
◎ Eccles. 3:1–8 (There is a time for every purpose under heaven.)

NOTES

Use the space below to jot notes and reminders for the next time you use this strategy.

Trees of Life

OVERVIEW In this strategy the young people explore the family genealogy of Jesus.

Suggested Time

30 to 45 minutes

Group Size

This strategy can be done with no more than ten young people. If your group is larger, divide it up and recruit an adult helper to lead each smaller group through the strategy.

Materials Needed

- ☼ newsprint
- ☼ masking tape
- ☼ a black and a red marker
- ☼ drawing paper, one sheet for each person
- ☼ pencils
- ☼ Bibles, one for every two people
- ☼ red pencils or thin-line markers, one for each person
- ☼ 12-inch-long pieces of yarn, one for each person

PROCEDURE

Preparation. Draw three simple trees side by side on a large piece of newsprint. At the bottom of the first tree, where the tree's roots would be, write your name. Above your name, to the left of the trunk, write your father's name. Above your name, to the right of the trunk, write your mother's name. Above their names write the names of their fathers and mothers. Above those names write the names of their grandfathers and grandmothers. Continue up the tree, writing your ancestors' names as far back in history as you can remember.

At the bottom of the second tree, where the roots would be, write the name of Jesus. At the bottom of the third tree, where the roots would be, write the name of Jesus again. Post the newsprint in the front of your room.

1. When you are ready to begin, gather the young people by the newsprint that you posted. Point out your family tree and read the names on it. Tell the young people one funny or neat thing you can remember about one of your grandparents or great-grandparents.

2. Distribute drawing paper and a pencil to everyone. Invite them each to draw three trees side by side on their piece of paper. Have them write their name under the first tree and the name of Jesus under both of the other trees.

Above their name on the first tree, to the left of the trunk, have them write their father's name. Above their name, to the right of the trunk, have them write their mother's name. Invite them to write the names of their grandparents and great-grandparents and any other ancestors they can remember above their parents' names. Explain that this is their genealogy, or family tree.

3. Explain that you are now going to explore the genealogy of Jesus. Over the second tree on the posted newsprint, write the heading, "According to Matthew—Abraham." Over the third tree, write the heading, "According to Luke—Adam." Invite the young people to do the same on their paper. Divide the large group into pairs and distribute a Bible to each pair.

Tell the young people to find Matt. 1:16. Ask for a volunteer to find the names of Jesus' parents according to Matthew. On the second tree, they should write, "Joseph," to the left of the trunk and, "Mary," to the right. Do the same on the posted newsprint. Now ask them to identify the name of the grandfather of Jesus and write, "Jacob," above Joseph's name. Tell them to continue writing the names from the genealogy for five or six generations back. Do the same on the posted newsprint.

Draw a red box above Mary's name on the newsprint. Inside the box write, "Joachim, Anne (known by tradition)." Distribute red pencils or thin-line markers and invite the young people to do the same on their paper. Explain that we know these names because of word of mouth, or oral tradition, that has been passed down from generation to generation of Catholic Christian people.

4. Now invite the young people to turn to Luke 3:23 and find the names of Jesus' parents. They will find only Joseph. Explain to the young people that Luke traces only Joseph's side of the family. If the young people ask why, explain that in the time of Jesus, inheritance was given only to the sons through their father's side of the family. Tell them to continue writing the genealogy of Luke for five or six generations back. Do the same on the newsprint.

Encourage the young people to discuss the differences they find between their genealogy and the genealogies of Jesus. They will probably notice that they can trace both sides of their family back at least three generations and that there is not a record of both sides of Jesus' family according to either Matthew or Luke.

5. Ask the young people to compare the genealogies from Luke and Matthew. They will notice that Matthew's genealogy goes back to Abraham, and Luke's genealogy goes back to Adam. Explain that this information shows us that we do not have an accurate genealogy of Jesus and that the Bible gives us only clues to Jesus' background and roots.

6. Distribute 12-inch-long pieces of yarn to everyone. Tell them to roll up their genealogy paper and tie it closed with the piece of yarn. Invite them to take their genealogy paper home and save it until Christmastime. Tell them that they should tie it as an ornament on their Christmas tree as a reminder that even while we celebrate the birth of Jesus, we know little about his historical life.

7. Have your group stand in a circle. Go around the circle and invite each person to state the name of one of her or his ancestors, as you pray the following prayer:

Jesus, our brother, we pray for _____ [have each person name an ancestor]. May all these people who gave us our roots be a reminder of your teachings. We honor them as we honor you. Amen.

ALTERNATIVE APPROACHES

⌾ If you have time, expand the comparison of genealogies in step 4. Urge the young people to look for other differences, such as these:
  ◉ One of them names some women, the other does not.
  ◉ The names of Joseph's ancestors are different in each one.
  Ask the young people to speculate why this is so. (Accept any plausible explanations.)
⌾ Instead of having everyone complete both genealogies for Jesus, assign the genealogy of Matthew to half of your group and the genealogy of Luke to the other half. Let the young people write the names as far back as they have room for on their paper. After they have completed the genealogies, pair off

those who did Matthew's genealogy with those who did Luke's genealogy. Have them compare the two genealogies. Recruit a volunteer to name some of the differences. Explain that the differences are intentional and that they show us that we do not have an accurate history of Jesus' family.

 Bring in a potted tree or a large tree branch in a planter. Instruct the young people to write the names of Jesus' ancestors on separate 3-by-5-inch cards. Tell them to punch a hole in one corner of each card. Have them string yarn through the hole to make a hanger. Invite them to take turns hanging the cards on the tree or branch. Invite one of the young people to make a sign out of a piece of poster board that states, "The genealogy of Jesus: a family mystery." Have him or her put the sign on the tree or branch. Gather your group around the tree or branch while you read the following words:

> He was a human just like you. He had parents who loved him and who worried about him. He probably visited his grandparents during holidays. They were probably very proud of him. His roots were made up of people who were very religious and who had a rich tradition of prayer. He learned their lessons well because he grew up to be a man of prayer. He was human just like you, and just like you he had a wonderful family tree, but it does not tell us the whole story!

NOTES

Use the space below to jot notes and reminders for the next time you use this strategy.

Fortune Cookies Prayers

OVERVIEW

In this strategy the young people write four varieties of prayers to be used at a family dinner.

Suggested Time

25 to 30 minutes

Group Size

This strategy is best done with a group no larger than twenty. If your group is larger than that, divide it up and recruit an adult helper to lead each smaller group through the strategy.

Materials Needed

- 1-by-3-inch strips of paper, four for each person
- fortune cookies, four for each person
- a box of toothpicks
- pens or pencils
- resealable plastic bags, one for each person
- Bibles, one for every two people
- newsprint and a marker
- masking tape

PROCEDURE

Preparation. Write the following list on a piece of newsprint and post it in your meeting room:

Passages that illustrate four styles of prayer
Petition: Ps. 86:1–7
Thanksgiving: Ps. 107:1–2
Praise: Zeph. 3:14–18
Lament: Lamentations, chapter 5

1. When you are ready to begin, distribute to each person four 1-by-3-inch strips of paper, four fortune cookies, some toothpicks, a pen or pencil, and a resealable plastic bag.

Direct the young people to label one strip of paper, "Petition," another, "Thanksgiving," the third one, "Praise," and the fourth one, "Lament."

Divide the group into pairs and give each pair a Bible. Point out the Bible passages that you posted on newsprint and instruct the young people to look them up as they are read. Read the passages aloud or have a volunteer read them. Explain to the young people that the passages illustrate four different kinds of prayer. Name the four kinds again: petition, thanksgiving, praise, and lament.

Invite the young people to consider their own life and think of some favor they need from God or something they want to ask of God. Tell them that they can ask God for this favor in a prayer of petition. Direct them to compose a prayer and write it on the paper that they labeled "Petition." Have them use this formula:

 O God, grant that _____ [insert the prayer request].

For example, a prayer of petition might read, "O God, grant that we have peace on earth." Have them use a toothpick to carefully stuff this paper into the opening of one of the fortune cookies.

Now invite them to think of something in their life for which they are grateful. On the small paper labeled "Thanksgiving," have them write a prayer of thanksgiving, using this formula:

O God, I am thankful for _____ [insert something for which you are thankful].

Have them use a toothpick to carefully stuff this paper into the opening of another fortune cookie.

Have them consider how they might express praise to God in a prayer. Tell them to write that prayer on the piece of paper that they have labeled "Praise," using this formula:

O God, I praise you for _____ [insert something that you would like to praise].

Invite them to carefully stuff that paper into another fortune cookie.

Finally, ask the young people to consider some terrible tragedy or event in their life or in the world. Tell them to compose a short prayer that complains to or questions God about why this event happened. Explain that this complaining or questioning is a prayer of lament. Have them write the prayer on the paper labeled "Lament." Direct them to carefully stuff this paper into their last fortune cookie.

Tell the young people to place their four cookies in their plastic bag and to take the fortune cookies home and use them as a table prayer at a family dinner. Instruct them to explain to their family that four different kinds of prayers are in the cookies and that each one is to be broken out of the cookie and read as a part of the family's meal prayer (disregard the original fortunes in the cookies).

2. Invite the group to stand in a circle. Have everyone extend their hands forward with their palms up and with their bag of cookies resting in their palms. Close with the following prayer or one you spontaneously compose using a similar theme:

 We hold our prayers before you, O God. Hear us as we lament, as we sing your praises. May our words of thanksgiving express our gratitude for your gifts. We know that only you can answer our prayers and petitions. We place our trust in you, and we ask this in your name, O Holy One. Amen.

ALTERNATIVE APPROACHES

◎ Invite the young people to select a family member whom they feel needs prayers and have them write the fortune cookie prayers specifically for that person. Tell them to give the cookies to the person they select, letting that person find the prayers as a surprise.

◎ If you have time, invite the young people to write blessing prayers for their family members and to place them in two or three extra fortune cookies. For example, they might write a prayer in which they request God's blessings on their mother. Invite the young people to think of creative ways to hide the cookies, such as in a family member's briefcase, a sack lunch, a book bag, or a desk drawer.

◎ Instead of stuffing the prayers into the fortune cookies, have the young people attach them to the cookies using small rubber bands.

◎ If you cannot get fortune cookies, bake or buy any kind of cookie. Provide each person with four resealable plastic bags and eight cookies. Tell the young people to place in each bag one of their prayers with two cookies. Suggest that they take the bags home to use in any of the ways suggested above.

SCRIPTURAL CONNECTIONS

◎ Matt. 27:46–50 (Jesus laments that God has forsaken him.)
◎ Mark 14:34–36 (Jesus petitions God to have pity on him.)
◎ Luke 2:25–32 (Simeon prays in thanksgiving for the honor of seeing the Messiah.)
◎ John 17:1–7 (Jesus gives praise that God has entrusted him with a message of truth and love.)

NOTES

Use the space below to jot notes and reminders for the next time you use this strategy.

Singing Prayers

OVERVIEW

This activity has the young people use the Psalms as a guide to writing a prayer for a family member.

Suggested Time

15 to 20 minutes

Group Size

This strategy can be done with any size group.

Materials Needed

- ☼ copies of handout 4, "A Short-Stack of Psalms," one for each person
- ☼ envelopes, five for each person
- ☼ pens
- ☼ scissors, one for each person
- ☼ packages of colored thin-line markers, one for every three or four people
- ☼ a Bible
- ☼ a candle and matches

PROCEDURE

Preparation. Place a Bible and a candle at the front of your room. Open the Bible to the beginning of the Book of Psalms.

1. When you are ready to begin, give each person a copy of handout 4, five envelopes, a scissors, and a pen.

Explain in your own words how the Psalms were written as songs and that they express a full range of human emotions. Tell your group that the Hebrew people used the Psalms as songs and prayers.

Read aloud the psalms from the handout.

2. Tell the young people to cut apart the psalms and to lay out the five pieces of paper with the psalms in front of them so that they can easily see each one.

Invite the young people to think about their family members. Ask them to consider and identify a family member who has a problem of some kind, one who needs a word of comfort, someone who is ill, someone who is elderly, and one who has had a good thing happen recently. Tell the young people to match each psalm to the family member they have identified as most in need of that psalm and to write that person's name in the space provided below the psalm citation.

After they have labeled each psalm with the name of one of their family members, distribute packages of colored thin-line markers. Instruct the young people to decorate their psalms with the markers. Let them work in groups of three or four so that they can share the markers.

Tell the young people to put each of their five psalms into a separate envelope and to write on the envelope the name of the person the psalm is for. Have the young people put their envelopes on the Bible that you set out.

3. Close by lighting a candle and holding up the Bible. Read the following prayer or one that you compose:

O God of all goodness, we place our psalm prayers before you. Please help the family members we have selected as recipients of these prayers. May they remember that you have promised never to leave them alone. In that assurance we pray. Amen!

Let the young people come forward to reclaim their envelopes and tell them that during the next week, they should either mail or deliver the psalms to the family members they selected.

ALTERNATIVE APPROACHES

◎ Instead of using the handout as the only source for the psalms, have the young people pair off and search the Book of Psalms for other psalms that would be appropriate as prayers for their family members.

◎ Invite the young people to read their chosen psalms aloud to their family members or to copy the psalms into e-mail messages and send them to the selected family members.

◎ If you have time, invite the young people to work together to put one of the psalms on the handout to music. Have them think of the melody of a simple nursery rhyme or a popular song and to fit the words of the psalm to the music. Tell them that they can rearrange the words, add words, or rewrite the psalm in their own words in order to facilitate putting it to music.

NOTES

Use the space below to jot notes and reminders for the next time you use this strategy.

A Short-Stack of Psalms

A Psalm in Time of Conflict

Psalm 7:4–18

For _____

Lᴏʀᴅ my God, if I am at fault in this,
    if there is guilt on my hands,
If I have repaid my friend with evil—
· · · · · · · · · · · ·
Then let my enemy pursue and overtake me.
· · · · · · · · · · · ·

Grant me justice, Lᴏʀᴅ, for I am blameless,
    free of any guilt.
Bring the malice of the wicked to an end;
· · · · · · · · · · · ·
O God of justice,
    who tries hearts and minds.
· · · · · · · · · · · ·
I praise the justice of the Lᴏʀᴅ;
    I celebrate the name of the Lᴏʀᴅ Most High.

                      (NAB)

A Psalm of Comfort

Psalm 23:1–4

For _____

The Lᴏʀᴅ is my shepherd,
    there is nothing I lack.
In green pastures you let me graze;
    to safe waters you lead me;
· · · · · · · · · · · ·
You guide me along the right path
    for the sake of your name.
Even when I walk through a dark valley,
    I fear no harm for you are at my side;
    your rod and staff give me courage.

                      (NAB)

A Psalm for Healing

Psalm 38:7–23

For _____

I am stooped and deeply bowed;
    all day I go about mourning.
My loins burn with fever;
    my flesh is afflicted.
I am numb and utterly crushed;
    I wail with anguish of heart.
My Lord, my deepest yearning is before you;
    my groaning is not hidden from you.
My heart shudders, my strength forsakes me;
    the very light of my eyes has failed.

. . . .

Come quickly to help me,
    my Lord and my salvation!

(NAB)

A Psalm of Thanks

Psalm 148:1–13

For _____

Hallelujah!

Praise the LORD from the heavens;
    give praise in the heights.

. . . .

You kings of the earth and all peoples,
    princes and all who govern on earth;
Young men and women too,
    old and young alike.
Let them all praise the LORD's name,
    for [the Lord's] name alone is exalted.

(NAB)

A Psalm for an Elder

Psalm 71:17–22

For _____

God, you have taught me from my youth,
    to this day I proclaim your wondrous deeds.
Now that I am old and gray,
    do not forsake me, God,
That I may proclaim your might
    to all generations yet to come.

. . . .

You have sent me many bitter afflictions,
    but once more revive me.
From the watery depths of the earth
    once more you raise me up.

. . . .

That I may praise you with the lyre
    for your faithfulness, my God,
And sing to you with the harp!

(NAB)

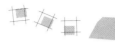

Appendix 1
Connections to the Discovering Program by HELP Strategy

"Dare to Share"

This strategy complements the following courses in the Discovering Program:
- *Learning to Communicate*
- *Understanding Myself*

"What Is That You Said?"

This strategy complements the following courses in the Discovering Program:
- *Learning to Communicate*
- *Understanding Myself*

"Decisions! Decisions!"

This strategy complements the following courses in the Discovering Program:
- *Learning to Communicate*
- *Making Decisions*

"Birth Order"

This strategy complements the following course in the Discovering Program:
- *Understanding Myself*

"Back-to-Back"

This strategy complements the following course in the Discovering Program:
- *Learning to Communicate*

"Traveling Friends Dinner"

This strategy complements the following courses in the Discovering Program:
- *Becoming Friends*
- *Gathering to Celebrate*

"Serve Others Day"

This strategy may be used with any course in the Discovering Program, especially the following one:
- *Seeking Justice*

"Love Is Heart Work"

This strategy complements the following courses in the Discovering Program:
- *Becoming Friends*
- *Exploring the Bible*
- *Learning to Communicate*

"Faith Connecting"

This strategy complements the following courses in the Discovering Program:
- *Being Catholic*
- *Learning to Communicate*
- *Understanding Myself*

"A Celebration of Culture"

This strategy complements the following courses in the Discovering Program:
- *Being Catholic*
- *Understanding Myself*

"A Mother-Daughter and Father-Son Gathering About Sexuality"

This strategy complements the following courses in the Discovering Program:
- *Growing Up Sexually*
- *Learning to Communicate*
- *Understanding Myself*

"Birthday Blessings"

This strategy complements the following courses in the Discovering Program:
- *Learning to Communicate*
- *Understanding Myself*

"Count Your Blessings"

This strategy complements the following course in the Discovering Program:
- *Seeking Justice*

"Prayers of Fire and Water"

This strategy complements the following course in the Discovering Program:
- *Praying*

"Suits You"

This strategy complements the following courses in the Discovering Program:
- *Learning to Communicate*
- *Meeting Jesus*
- *Understanding Myself*

"Post Your Beliefs"

This strategy complements the following courses in the Discovering Program:
- *Being Catholic*
- *Learning to Communicate*
- *Praying*

"Photo Gallery"

This strategy complements the following courses in the Discovering Program:
- *Being Catholic*
- *Celebrating the Eucharist*
- *Gathering to Celebrate*
- *Understanding Myself*

"Sharing Tough Times"

This strategy complements the following courses in the Discovering Program:
- *Dealing with Tough Times*
- *Learning to Communicate*

"Table Fable"

This strategy complements the following courses in the Discovering Program:
- *Learning to Communicate*
- *Making Decisions*
- *Understanding Myself*

"Trees of Life"

This strategy complements the following courses in the Discovering Program:
- *Exploring the Bible*
- *Meeting Jesus*
- *Understanding Myself*

"Fortune Cookies Prayers"

This strategy may be used with any course in the Discovering program, especially the following two:
- *Exploring the Bible*
- *Praying*

"Singing Prayers"

This strategy complements the following courses in the Discovering Program:
- *Exploring the Story of Israel*
- *Praying*

Appendix 2

Connections to the Discovering Program by Discovering Course

Becoming Friends

The following HELP strategies complement this course:
◎ "Traveling Friends Dinner"
◎ "Love Is Heart Work"

Being Catholic

The following HELP strategies complement this course:
◎ "A Celebration of Culture"
◎ "Faith Connecting"
◎ "Post Your Beliefs"
◎ "Photo Gallery"

Celebrating the Eucharist

The following HELP strategy complements this course:
◎ "Photo Gallery"

Dealing with Tough Times

The following HELP strategy complements this course:
- ◎ "Sharing Tough Times"

Exploring the Bible

The following HELP strategies complement this course:
- ◎ "Love Is Heart Work"
- ◎ "Trees of Life"
- ◎ "Fortune Cookies Prayers"

Exploring the Story of Israel

The following HELP strategy complements this course:
- ◎ "Singing Prayers"

Gathering to Celebrate

The following HELP strategies complement this course:
- ◎ "Photo Gallery"
- ◎ "Traveling Friends Dinner"

Growing Up Sexually

The following HELP strategy complements this course:
- ◎ "A Mother-Daughter and Father-Son Gathering About Sexuality"

Learning to Communicate

The following HELP strategies complement this course:
- ◎ "Dare to Share"
- ◎ "What Is That You Said?"
- ◎ "Decisions! Decisions!"
- ◎ "Back-to-Back"
- ◎ "Love Is Heart Work"
- ◎ "Faith Connecting"
- ◎ "A Mother-Daughter and Father-Son Gathering About Sexuality"
- ◎ "Birthday Blessings"
- ◎ "Suits You"
- ◎ "Post Your Beliefs"
- ◎ "Sharing Tough Times"
- ◎ "Table Fable"

Making Decisions

The following HELP strategies complement this course:
- "Decisions! Decisions!"
- "Table Fable"

Meeting Jesus

The following HELP strategies complement this course:
- "Suits You"
- "Trees of Life"

Praying

The following HELP strategies complement this course:
- "Prayers of Fire and Water"
- "Post Your Beliefs"
- "Fortune Cookies Prayers"
- "Singing Prayers"

Seeking Justice

The following HELP strategies complement this course:
- "Serve Others Day"
- "Count Your Blessings"

Understanding Myself

The following HELP strategies complement this course:
- "Dare to Share"
- "What Is That You Said?"
- "Birth Order"
- "Faith Connecting"
- "A Celebration of Culture"
- "A Mother-Daughter and Father-Son Gathering About Sexuality"
- "Birthday Blessings"
- "Suits You"
- "Photo Gallery"
- "Table Fable"
- "Trees of Life"

Acknowledgments *(continued)*

The scriptural quotations marked NAB are from the New American Bible with revised Psalms and revised New Testament. Copyright © 1991, 1986, and 1970 by the Confraternity of Christian Doctrine, 3211 Fourth Street NE, Washington, DC 20017. All rights reserved.

All other scriptural quotations contained herein are from the New Revised Standard Version of the Bible. Copyright © 1989 by the Division of Christian Education of the National Council of the Churches of Christ in the United States of America. All rights reserved.

The scriptural material described as adapted or based on is freely paraphrased and is not to be used or understood as an official translation of the Bible.

The Apostles' Creed on handout 3 is from the *Catechism of the Catholic Church,* by the Libreria Editrice Vaticana, translated by the United States Catholic Conference (USCC) (Washington, DC: USCC, 1994), pages 49–50. English translation copyright © 1994 by the USCC—Libreria Editrice Vaticana.